Contents

Introduction 5

Chapter One
The Early Years 7

Chapter Two
Expansion 25

Chapter Three
Extermination through Labour 57

Chapter Four
Auschwitz 75

Chapter Five
Liberated 99

Appendix I
List of Concentration Camps and Sub-Camps . . . 113

Appendix II
Auschwitz Sub-Camps 123

IMAGES OF WAR
HIMMLER'S SLAVE LABOUR CAMPS

RARE PHOTOGRAPHS FROM WARTIME ARCHIVES

Ian Baxter

Pen & Sword
MILITARY

About the Author

Ian Baxter is a military historian who specialises in German twentieth-century military history. He has written more than seventy books, including *Poland: The Eighteen-Day Victory March*; *Panzers in North Africa*; *The Waffen-SS Ardennes Offensive*; *The Western Campaign*; *The 12th SS Panzer Division Hitlerjugend*; *Waffen-SS on the Western Front*; *Waffen-SS on the Eastern Front*; *The Red Army at Stalingrad*; *Elite German Forces of World War II*; *Armoured Warfare: German Tanks of World War II*; *Blitzkrieg*; *Panzer Divisions at War*; *German Armoured Vehicles of World War Two*; *Last Two Years of the Waffen-SS at War*; *German Soldier Uniforms and Insignia*; *German Guns of the Third Reich*; *From Retreat to Defeat: The Last Years of the German Army at War 1943–45* and, most recently, *The Sixth Army and the Road to Stalingrad*.

He has written over a hundred articles, including 'Last days of Hitler', 'Wolf's Lair', 'The Story of the V1 and V2 Rocket Programme', 'Secret Aircraft of World War Two', 'Rommel at Tobruk', 'Hitler's War with his Generals', 'Secret British Plans to Assassinate Hitler', 'The SS at Arnhem', 'Hitlerjugend', 'Battle of Caen 1944', 'Gebirgsjäger at War', 'Panzer Crews', 'Hitlerjugend Guerrillas', 'Last Battles in the East', 'The Battle of Berlin' and many more.

He has also reviewed numerous military studies for publication, supplied thousands of photographs and important documents to various publishers and film production companies worldwide, and he lectures to schools, colleges and universities throughout the United Kingdom and the Republic of Ireland.

First published in Great Britain in 2025 by
PEN & SWORD MILITARY
an imprint of Pen & Sword Books Ltd
Yorkshire – Philadelphia

Copyright © Ian Baxter, 2025

ISBN 978-1-03610-339-2

The right of Ian Baxter to be identified as the author of this work has been asserted by him in accordance with the Copyright, Designs and Patents Act 1988.

A CIP catalogue record for this book is available from the British Library.

All rights reserved. No part of this book may be reproduced, transmitted, downloaded, decompiled or reverse engineered in any form or by any means, electronic or mechanical including photocopying, recording or by any information storage and retrieval system, without permission from the Publisher in writing. No part of this book may be used or reproduced in any manner for the purpose of training artificial intelligence technologies or systems.

Typeset by Concept, Huddersfield, West Yorkshire, HD4 5JL.
Printed and bound in England by CPI Group (UK) Ltd, Croydon, CR0 4YY.

The Publisher's authorised representative in the EU for product safety is Authorised Rep Compliance Ltd, Ground Floor, 71 Lower Baggot Street, Dublin D02 P593, Ireland – www.arccompliance.com

For a complete list of Pen & Sword titles please contact
PEN & SWORD BOOKS LTD
47 Church Street, Barnsley, South Yorkshire, S70 2AS, England
E-mail: enquiries@pen-and-sword.co.uk
Website: www.pen-and-sword.co.uk
or
PEN & SWORD BOOKS
1950 Lawrence Road, Havertown, PA 19083, USA
E-mail: uspen-and-sword@casematepublishers.com
Website: www.penandswordbooks.com

Introduction

Shortly after their rise to power, the Nazis established specific *Arbeitslager* (labour camps) which housed *Ostarbeiter* (Eastern workers), *Fremdarbeiter* (other foreign workers) and sundry forced labourers who were rounded up and brought in from the East. These were distinct from the SS-run concentration camps.

The use of forced labour grew significantly in 1937 due to rearmament requirements and again after the outbreak of war. The invasion of the Soviet Union in June 1941 further heightened demands for labour and the availability of new workers in areas under Nazi occupation. Vast numbers were deported to forced labour camps where they worked either in the production of war materials or on construction projects. Due to the Nazis' view that inmates were slaves pure and simple and were replaceable with others, there was complete disregard for the health of the prisoners. Required to work long hours with little or no time for rest or breaks, they suffered from insufficiencies of food, equipment, medicine and clothing. As a result of these conditions and brutal treatment, their death rates were shockingly high. By 1945 more than 14 million people had been exploited in the network of hundreds of forced labour camps that stretched across Nazi-occupied Europe. In true Images of War series style, this superbly illustrated book graphically describes the growth of the slave labour camp system and the conditions inflicted on the luckless labour force.

Chapter One

The Early Years

'*Arbeit Macht Frei*' – 'Work Sets You Free'
The first concentration camps were erected in Germany in February 1933, and these camps were primarily used to house and torture political opponents and union organizers. The camps held some 45,000 prisoners and during the mid- to late-1930s these camps were greatly expanded. When *SS-Reichsführer* Heinrich Himmler took control of the concentration camp system throughout Germany he started using the camps' facilities and personnel to purge German society of so-called racially undesirable elements such as Jews, criminals, homosexuals, Jehovah's Witnesses, gypsies and any other elements deemed a threat to Nazi rule.

After March 1938 when Nazi Germany annexed Austria there were more arrests and thousands of German and Austrian Jews were arrested and detained in camps such as Dachau, Buchenwald and Sachsenhausen.

By 1939 Nazi government officials were demanding immediate action with the expansion of the concentration camp system throughout Germany and its newly conquered territory of Poland. As a result the German authorities began planning and building various camps where those arrested could be incarcerated and set to work as stonebreakers and construction workers for buildings and streets. Himmler envisaged that these people would remain as a slave labour force, and it was therefore deemed necessary to erect these so-called 'quarantine camps' in order to subdue the local population. Initially it had been proposed that the 'quarantine camps' were to hold the prisoners until they were sent to the various other concentration camps within the Reich. However, it soon became apparent that this purpose was totally impractical so approval was granted for these camps to function as a permanent prison for all those sent there.

Throughout the Reich and newly captured territories thousands of concentration camps were built across Europe with some of them being constructed by the inmates themselves. The Nazi concentration camp system itself was run by the Concentration Camps Inspectorate and later the SS Main Economic and Administrative Office. The Inspectorate employed various types of camps which were either work or death camps or were run as a dual-function slave labour camp and murder facility. These camps comprised civilian workers' camps, custody camps, civilian internment camps, camps for Jews, forced labour camps, penal punishment camps, prisoner-of-war camps, satellite camps, transit camps, youth detention camps, extermination camps and slave labour and murder camps.

One of the earliest camps constructed was Dachau. Himmler regarded this new camp as the foundation for all other camps. It was the first regular concentration camp established by the National Socialist government and was the first camp for political opponents who were seen as an imminent threat to the new German government. Dachau was established on 20 March 1933, and it served as a prototype and model for the other concentration camps that followed. Its basic organization, the camp layout and the construction of buildings was developed and ordered by *SS-Brigadeführer* Theodor Eicke, who was regarded as the director and architect of the concentration camp system.

Dachau was not like a prison. Unlike in normal prisons, the inmates did not know how long their sentence would run. Effectively they led a permanent existence of uncertainty as to when they might regain their freedom. Also life for the prisoners inside Dachau was brutal. The SS guards were all ordered to follow Eicke's demand for blind and absolute obedience and to treat each prisoner with fanatical hatred. The commandant was also a great believer that the inmates were able to endure prison with more discipline if they were allowed to work. To him, working while enslaved was a kind of mystical declaration that self-sacrifice through endless labour brought about some sort of spiritual freedom. It was this slogan and ardent belief that prompted Eicke to display the inscription '*Arbeit Macht Frei*' ('Works Sets You Free') on the main entrance gate of Dachau. This slogan itself was not new to the National Socialists.

As Inspector of Concentration Camps Eicke soon established a permanent camp system including notorious places such as Sachsenhausen and Buchenwald. Eicke based Sachsenhausen on the 'Dachau model' that he himself had created. The brutal methods of mistreating prisoners were applied along with Dachau's harsh disciplinary and punishment regulations including the death penalty and punishment by the whip. As with Dachau, solitary confinement, general physical abuse and forced labour became standard practice.

By the late 1930s Nazi foreign policy had become increasingly aggressive. Eicke made it clear to his men that the threat of war meant that an expansion of the SS would provide greater internal security and as a consequence the concentration camps would flourish with new intakes of prisoners. Himmler had already envisaged an expansion programme, but this would not include Eicke. Although Eicke was allowed to retain command of the camps and the new *SS-Verfügungstruppe* (Special Service Troops), all policy matters concerning the *SS-Totenkopfverbände* (Death's Head Battalions) would be run at the highest level between Himmler and the Führer Adolf Hitler.

A portrait photograph of Theodor Eicke, here in the rank of *SS-Obergruppenführer* and General of the Waffen-SS. Eicke had been made commander of Dachau concentration camp in June 1933 and became a major figure in the SS. He was regarded as the architect, builder and director of the concentration camp system and ruled the prisoners there with an iron fist.

Prisoners' barracks in the Dachau concentration camp. The camp was opened on 22 March 1933 and was initially constructed to hold political prisoners comprising communists, social democrats and other people regarded as a threat or hostile to the Nazis. The camp was located on the grounds of an abandoned munitions factory north-east of the medieval town of Dachau and north-west of Munich. Once the camp was opened Himmler ordered the expansion of the camp to include forced labour. Eventually Jews, Romani, German and Austrian criminals and foreign nationals from countries occupied or invaded by Germany were incarcerated as well.

An infirmary in the Dachau concentration camp staffed by prisoners who had previously held occupations such as physicians or army surgeons. Life for the prisoners at the camp was lived in total fear of brutal treatment including floggings, standing cells and the so-called tree or pole hangings. Roll calls were also to be endured and inmates had to stand for considerably long periods. The entrance gate here was the first to carry the phrase 'Arbeit Macht Frei' ('Work Sets You Free'). Prisoners at the camp were originally sent as forced labour to a munitions factory and to expand the camp.

The first of two photographs showing an aerial view of the Dachau concentration camp.

As can be seen, the Dachau camp was extensive and had numerous buildings such as an administration centre containing offices for the Gestapo trial commissioner, SS authorities, the camp leader and his deputies. These administration offices consisted of large storage rooms for the personal belongings of prisoners, the roll-call square, the bunker, the canteen where prisoners served SS men with cigarettes and food, the camp office, the barracks, the infirmary and it even had a museum containing plaster images of prisoners who suffered from bodily defects.

A watch tower and section of the electric fence at the Dachau concentration camp. Although the camp initially focused on labour and re-education of the inmates, it soon shifted its policy to using forced labour as a method of torture and murder.

Jewish prisoners in Dachau harnessed to a steamroller in 1933.

(**Opposite, above**) Prisoners guarded by SA men line up in the yard of the Oranienburg concentration camp on the Havel River in Germany. In 1933 the camp was established in the centre of the town of Oranienburg on the main road to Berlin when the SA took over a disused brewery grounds. Prisoners were marched through the town to perform forced labour on behalf of the council.

(**Opposite, below**) SA guards overseeing prisoners during a work detail who were carrying a container near the entrance to the Oranienburg concentration camp. This camp housed some 3,000 prisoners and the inmates were totally suppressed by their captors. However, in 1936 the camp was closed and replaced in the area by the Sachsenhausen concentration camp.

(**Above**) Buchenwald prisoners at forced labour in Quarry II during 1937. The camp was built to hold 8,000 prisoners and was constructed to replace a number of nearby smaller concentration camps including Bad Sulza, Sachsenburg and Lichtenburg. The SS saw that Buchenwald would become a very profitable enterprise because of the nearby clay deposits where prisoners could be forced to work producing bricks. The first prisoners arrived on 15 July 1937 and had to clear the area of trees and erect numerous buildings. By September the population of the camp had increased to 2,400 following transfers from the other camps.

(**Opposite, above**) The first prisoners at Stutthof concentration camp eating during construction of the site. The camp was built purely to contain and murder what the SS regarded as Polish elite such as members of the intelligentsia, religious and political leaders. By November 1941 it had become a labour 'education camp' like Dachau and then the following year it was a regular concentration camp.

(**Opposite, below**) Stutthof prisoners involved in the construction of the camp queuing up for food. The first 150 inmates were imprisoned in early September 1939. The population of the camp soon rose to 6,000 during the following weeks as the German army advanced through Poland. By 1942 Jews comprised the most significant number of prisoners.

(**Above**) The road to Buchenwald concentration camp under construction. This road was nicknamed by the prisoners as the 'Blood Road' and was built to supply the new armaments factory in Buchenwald. The SS were ruthless and the road was built under terrible conditions during which prisoners were beaten and killed.

Six photographs showing prisoners from the Buchenwald concentration camp during forced labour constructing the Weimar-Buchenwald railway line. In the spring of 1943 Himmler ordered a 7-mile railway line to be laid connecting the Buchenwald concentration camp to the town of Weimar. The line did not start being used until the spring of 1944. However, it was not just freight trains that were used along the line but scheduled passenger trains as well including mass transports bringing Jews and other people detained by the Nazis who were no longer fit for labour at Auschwitz.

The prisoners' orchestra in Buchenwald concentration camp. Strange as it was, the SS at Buchenwald organized what was known as 'musical torture' in which inmates were forced into mass singing during the evening roll calls, often to the orchestra. Many of the inmates were already exhausted from a long day of forced labour, and singing was another way in which the guards could humiliate and punish the prisoners.

Dutch Jews wearing prison uniforms marked with a yellow star and the letter 'N' for Netherlands stand at attention during a roll call at the Buchenwald concentration camp.

A prisoner at forced labour splits wood in the Sachsenhausen concentration camp. Some 30,000 inmates died at the camp from brutal punishments, exhaustion through overwork, disease, malnutrition and pneumonia plus very poor living conditions. Many were executed or died as the result of some inhumane medical experiments.

A view of the prisoners' barracks in the Sachsenhausen concentration camp with Nazi slogans painted on the barracks. These barracks were built by the prisoners themselves. The camp itself grew in size over the years to almost 1,000 acres. Sachsenhausen mainly held Jews, gay men, Jehovah's Witnesses and political prisoners. By November 1939 the number of prisoners in the camp exceeded 11,300. Eventually a number of companies built factories close to the camp so that they could use the prisoners as slave labour. These included firms such as AEG, Siemens & Halske, Heinkel Flugzeugwerke, IG Farben and Daimler Benz Werke.

The Flossenbürg concentration camp. The camp was built in May 1938 and unlike many other camps built during this period it was constructed in a remote area in the Fichtel Mountains of Bavaria near the town of Flossenbürg. The camp's initial purpose was to make use of forced labour of prisoners for the production of granite for Nazi architecture. However, in 1943 the prisoners were switched to the production of Messerschmitt Bf 109 fighter aircraft.

Chapter Two

Expansion

Throughout the Reich and the occupied countries millions of Jews and other creeds regarded by the Germans as 'subhuman' were rounded up and herded into the various concentration camps. Those that were not indiscriminately shot or gassed in the T4 gas vans were forced to work in the many labour camps that were erected in Germany, Austria, France, Holland, Italy, Poland, Czechoslovakia, Lithuania, Latvia, Estonia, Norway and Finland.

Stutthof, east of the city of Danzig, was the first German concentration camp set up outside German borders and was in operation from 2 September 1939. Originally it was established as a civilian internment camp before its huge expansion programme. By November 1941 it had become a labour education camp similar to Dachau. The conditions on site under which the labour force had to work were appalling. Those unfortunate enough to be incarcerated in this camp had become slaves for the German Security Police and the machinery they were using was often a death trap. Much of their work was lethal and many inmates died, but some survived without permanent injury. Malnourished, badly equipped, lacking protective gear and constantly harassed by the guards, the workers had little chance of surviving their arduous labour.

During the operation of Stutthof in 1939 the Nazi authorities were able to exploit the labour of the prisoners across the concentration camp system for financial reward. During the invasion of Poland the war provided an opportunity to ban releases from the camps and provide the SS with a slave labour force. This gave the SS the chance to authorize the construction of new camps in the vicinity of factories such as the brickworks at Neuengamme or the stone quarry at Mauthausen. The materials extracted from these sites by the prisoners who endured such harsh forced labour were able to be sold to the Nazi authorities through SS-owned companies such as the German Earth and Stone Works.

The various people who were forced to work comprised political prisoners, resistance groups and those deemed sub-human such as Jews and Roma gypsies. The number of camps soon expanded in 1940 to include Gusen, Gross-Rosen and Auschwitz.

Life in these camps was brutal. Many of the inmates were constantly beaten with sticks or truncheons, there were shootings and every imaginable form of torture. Those who were ill or too weak to continue working were ordered to be shot in front of the work detail or were dragged away and executed. The other workers were compelled to continue working without pause until the foreman blew his whistle, ordering every man to lay down his tools. By the end of the day the majority of the men and women did not have the physical strength for further work. Many were on the point of collapsing, but those that had become too weak even to stand on their own two feet ran the risk the following morning of being declared unfit for further work and taken away. Those who had actually died on site from exhaustion or had been killed for some minor infringement earlier that day were piled up in heaps ready for collection by cart. Early the next morning the foreman would take stock of his workforce. Any person he deemed no longer able to perform to the satisfaction of the commandant was selected for death.

Those running the camps knew that the fear of being killed was enough to spur the workers on to greater efforts and undertake tasks beyond their physical strength. It was also noted that injured or ill workers regularly refrained from seeking medical treatment due to their terror of being executed. However, the death and injury rates of the construction gangs were mainly attributed to the guards physically abusing their work force.

In April 1941 the SS sent out orders to murder prisoners who were unable to work, especially those regarded as being racially inferior. Travelling SS doctors or camp personnel selected inmates who were exhausted or unwell and often sent them to euthanasia centres. This programme to murder the inmates of camps was one of numerous radical measures to kill people the Nazis deemed as being 'unworthy of life'. Although the operation was terminated by mid-1942 with the order for the 'Final Solution', as many as 20,000 people had been removed from the concentration camps and systematically killed. In the eyes of the SS, if camp inmates became sick, injured or were too weak to work, they were regarded as economically worthless. The prisoners across the whole concentration camp system were seen as expendable despite their increasing economic importance.

During the early part of the war while the concentration camp system was expanding, private sector cooperation still remained minimal. However, following the German invasion of Russia in June 1941 demands increased especially during the winter reverses later that year. Further camps were erected in order to compensate for the massive requirement needed in armaments. Himmler was fully aware that camps such as Auschwitz in Poland and Buchenwald in central Germany were important administrative centres for a huge network of forced labour camps. In addition to this, he knew it was vital that the SS-owned enterprises that encompassed the armament works along with private firms such as Junkers, Messerschmitt and IG Farben would increasingly rely almost exclusively on forced labour to dramatically increase wartime production. In fact the German electrical firm Siemens profited, as did a number of private companies, from the use of slave labour. As early as 1940 the company relied increasingly on forced labour in order to main production levels. A vast pool of prisoners was drafted in from areas conquered by the German military including Russian PoWs, Jews and Roma people. Some 80,000 labourers were forced to work at Siemens. Other companies included AEG which used large numbers of forced labourers as well as concentration camp prisoners under terrible conditions. Allianz in Berlin provided insurance facilities and they insured SS armaments factories, prisoners' barracks, material stores and vehicle fleets in camps including Auschwitz, Buchenwald and Dachau. There were also companies like BMW and Audi who employed forced labour. Continental was another company that relied on forced labour. They employed some 10,000 labourers and concentration camp detainees under inhumane conditions. In fact at Sachsenhausen concentration camp prisoners were forced to test new rubber shoe soles by walking around 25 miles each day. Some prisoners quickly became exhausted and were beaten or killed. Esso employed many forced labourers and PoWs from Poland, Ukraine and the Soviet Union in order to assist in oil production for the Reich and used a sub-camp of the Stutthof concentration camp located in Politz. Between 1940 and 1942 Lufthansa drafted in some 10,000 forced labourers including many children from occupied countries. The labourers were used to install and maintain radar systems which included assembling and maintaining aircraft. The forced labourers were housed and guarded in barracks run by Lufthansa on the Tempelhof sites and in numerous other locations in Berlin. During the early part of the war the German subsidiary of Ford was also engaged in vehicle and war production and employed slave/forced labour. Hugo Boss, an early supporter of the Nazis, drafted in thousands of slave labourers to manufacture the SS uniforms.

By 1942, as the war entered its third year, it was realized by the Nazis that a drastic increase in armaments was required in order to keep Germany on a proper war footing and an increase in forced labour was essential to accomplish this. In order to maintain high levels of war production including heavy industrialization and military industrial build-up there was an excessive increase in more private firms beginning to employ forced labour. During this period of expansion both the Wehrmacht and the Luftwaffe began to call for a vast assortment of weaponry specialized in diverse tasks in order to try to win the war. Despite the ballooning cost in terms of government resources the Nazis were unwilling to sacrifice expensive production runs for the sake of producing items that were inferior to the enemy's weaponry. As a consequence private firms felt compelled to employ forced labour in order to meet the stringent production requirements. The increased level of war production meant that more camps needed to be constructed quickly. As with the Nazis, all the private companies regarded the forced labourers as a commodity and the camps or special compounds where they lived were operated under appalling conditions. It was the equivalent of extermination through slavery.

(**Above**) A section of the barbed-wire fence and barracks in the Flossenbürg concentration camp. Many of the inmates were forced to work in the three nearby quarries. These quarries were made operational by the end of 1938 and a fourth opened in April 1941. All four quarries were located near the main camp and the granite was used for architectural purposes.

(**Opposite, above**) Prisoners at forced labour in the Wiener Graben quarry at the Mauthausen concentration camp. Initially Mauthausen served as a prison camp until 8 May 1939 when it was converted to a labour camp for political prisoners.

(**Opposite, below**) Spanish Republican prisoners can be seen here working in the quarry at the Mauthausen concentration camp. After the end of the Spanish Civil War, in 1939 the prison population ranged from 367,000 to 500,000 including soldiers and brigades of the Spanish Republican Army. Many republicans were transported to Himmler's concentration camp system where a large contingent was sent to work at Mauthausen. During 1939 the inmates were marched daily to the granite quarries at St Georgen/Gusen, which were more productive and more important than the Wiener Graben quarry.

A photograph taken in 1938 showing Sachsenhausen prisoners wearing uniforms with triangular badges standing in columns under the supervision of a camp guard. Some of these prisoners had to work in the much-feared penal satellite camp of Klinkerwerk, where the prisoners made bricks for the future development of Berlin. Some 2,000 of them were force-marched to the brickworks where they were compelled to work under brutal conditions.

New arrivals standing in front of what was nicknamed by the SS as the *Klagemauer* (the 'Wailing Wall') after a week-long trip in open railway cars to Mauthausen. By the autumn of 1941, it was not only Jews and political prisoners that were sent to the camp as Mauthausen also held large numbers of Russian PoWs. Separated from the other prisoners, they lived in exceptionally poor conditions with minimal or no shelter and hardly any food. Many of the prisoners subsequently died of exhaustion while working in the nearby quarries.

Prisoners carrying large stones up the 'stairs of death' (*Todesstiege*) from the Wiener Graben quarry at the Mauthausen concentration camp.

Two photographs showing the Wiener Graben quarry at the Mauthausen concentration camp.

The bodies of two Czech brothers who were shot in the Wiener Graben quarry at Mauthausen can be seen here face down in the grass on the side of the quarry road.

The quarry in the Flossenbürg concentration camp, which was nicknamed the 'death quarry' where thousands of inmates were forced to work. Owned by the German Earth and Stone Works, the prisoners, lacking proper clothing and safety precautions, were forced in all weathers to remove soil, blast out granite blocks and haul the massive rocks onto trolley wagons.

Seven photographs showing prisoners during forced labour in the Wiener Graben quarry at the Mauthausen concentration camp. Working in the quarry was brutal for the inmates. Himmler had introduced what he termed *Primitivbauweise* ('primitive construction'), in which prisoners were told to use only the most primitive tools and also, where possible, they should use their bare hands. To make conditions even harsher, the SS ordered the notorious *Kapos* and other guards to literally work the prisoners to death. In fact, the quarry was so terrible that even Auschwitz prisoners feared being sent there to work.

(**Below**) A collection of images showing Himmler's visit to Mauthausen concentration camp on 27 April 1941. He can be seen here with his entourage comprising people such as Ernst Kaltenbrunner, Franz Ziereis, Karl Chmielewski, August Eigruber and Georg Bachmayer. The Mauthausen camp was located on a hill overlooking the town of Mauthausen in Upper Austria, and it was the main camp of a group with some 100 further sub-camps located throughout Austria and southern Germany. By the time Himmler visited the camp, Mauthausen and its sub-camps had become one of the largest labour camp complexes in the German-controlled part of Europe. The visit also included Himmler touring the Wiener Graben quarry. Mauthausen and its sub-camps included quarries, munitions factories, mines and arms factories and later in the war also plants assembling the new Me 262 jet fighter. *(BA/Bender)*

SS-Hauptsturmführer Georg Bachmayer on the left is seen here posing for the camera at Mauthausen. The prisoners referred to Bachmayer as a brutal sadist. When he was not roaming the camp overseeing the work details he took part in meting out harsh punishments on the inmates who were sometimes too exhausted to work. He was often seen with his mastiff dogs that were particularly ferocious. Upon his command they would attack the workers, biting their bodies and sinking their sharp teeth into the victim's body and face, occasionally ripping them to pieces.

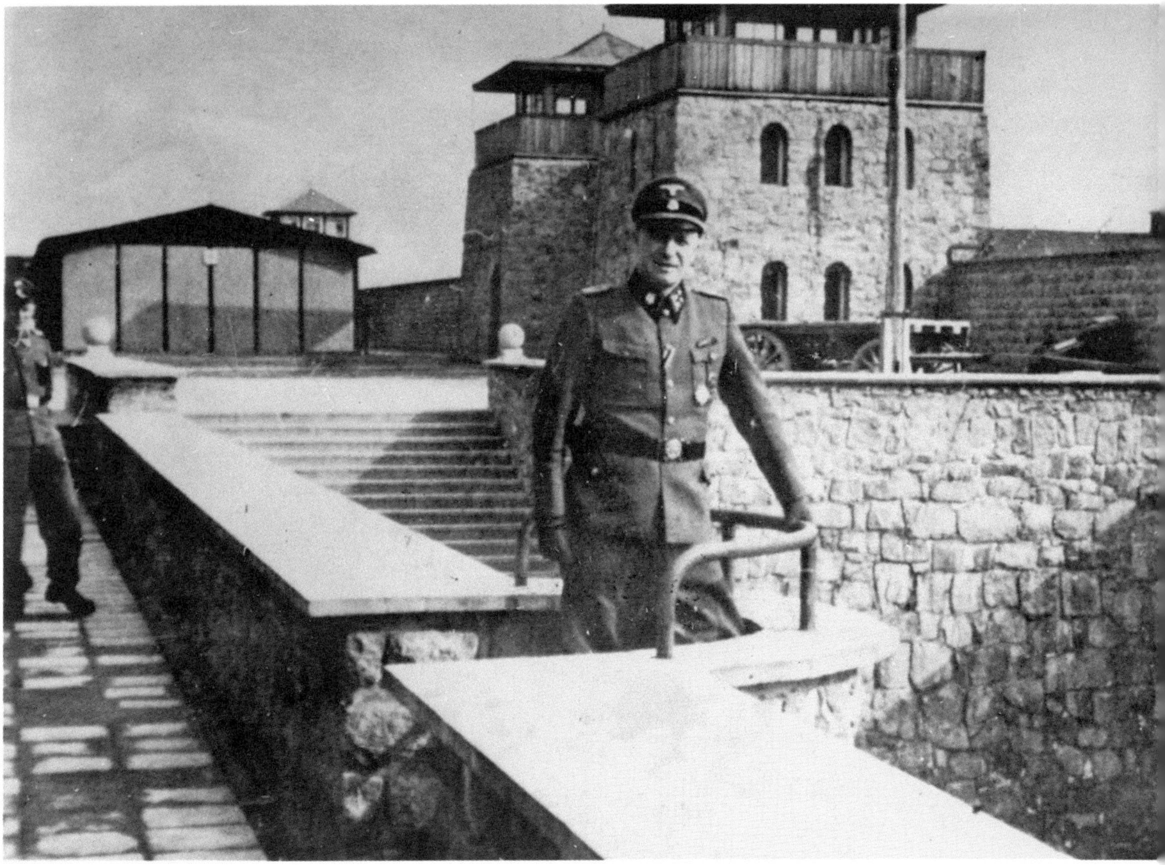

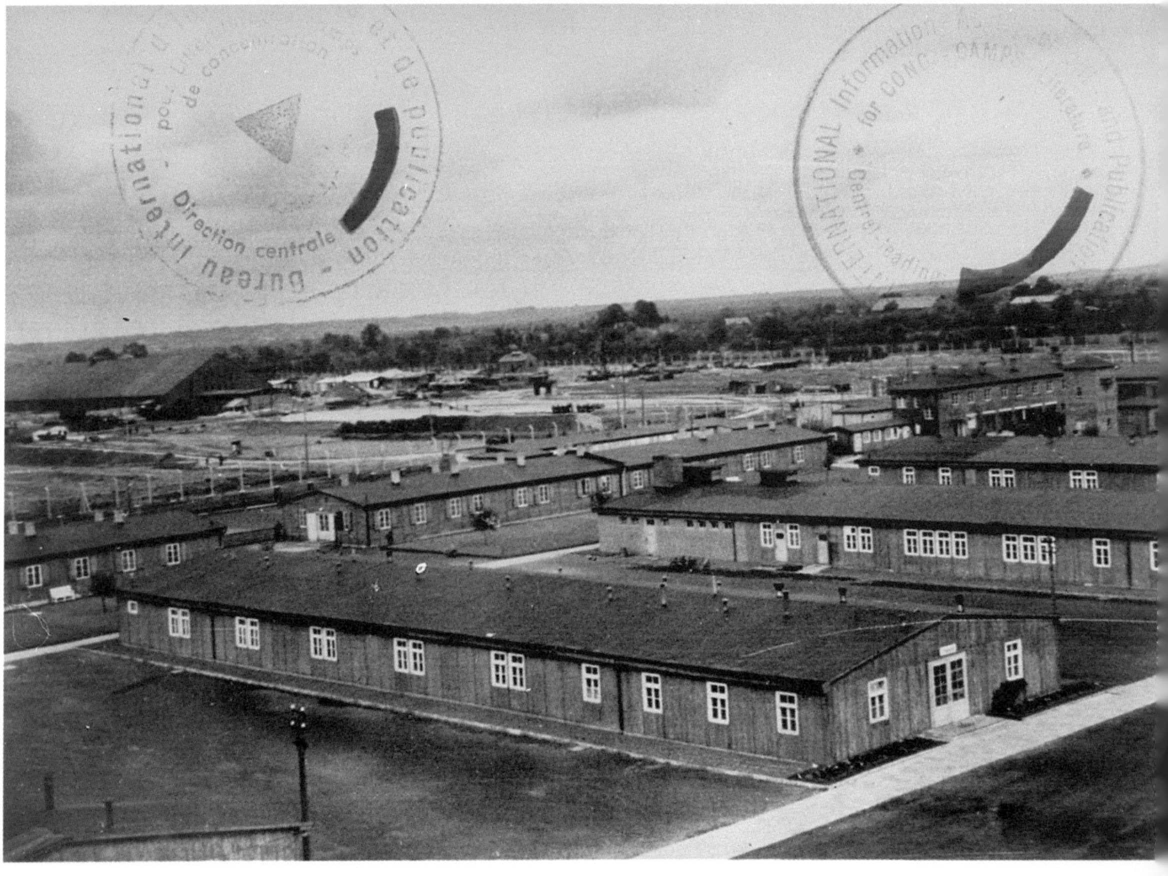
de concentration
Direction centrale
Bureau International
INTERNATIONAL Information
for CONC

(**Opposite, above**) *SS-Obersturmführer* Franz Ziereis poses in front of the commandant's headquarters on the wall overlooking the garage courtyard in Mauthausen. Under his command in June 1940 Mauthausen-Gusen had expanded to include not only larger main camps, but numerous satellite camps as well. In January 1941 the two main camps of Mauthausen-Gusen were designated Grade III facilities, the only two in the Reich system planned to house 'Incorrigible political enemies of the Reich', who were often classified as *Rückkehr Unerwünscht* ('Return Undesired'). He ruled the camp with an iron fist and used inmates for slave labour in numerous construction projects.

(**Opposite, below**) A view of the Neuengamme concentration camp. On the left is the camp brick factory. The camp was established in late 1938 as a sub-camp of the Sachsenhausen concentration camp. In April 1940 the SS signed a contract for a larger more modern brick factory for construction work for the city of Hamburg. During the camp's operations some 49,000 prisoners were sent to Sachsenhausen with 12,000 in Neuengamme and a further 37,000 in the sub-camps. It included some 10,000 women who were distributed in various sub-camps.

(**Above**) The interior of a barracks in the Flossenbürg concentration camp which was designed to house a staggering number of 1,500 prisoners. As the camp expanded, Flossenbürg became one of the main labour camps with almost eighty sub-camps. Twenty-seven sub-camps held female prisoners. The majority were sent to work and their chances of survival varied quite considerably.

Sachsenhausen prisoners wearing different types of uniforms eating a meal in the mess hall of the camp.

A view of prisoners in horse-drawn carts in the Mauthausen concentration camp.

A photograph showing concentration camp inmates hauling cartloads of earth for the construction of the 'Russian camp' of Mauthausen, which was the infirmary camp built by the SS in the autumn of 1941. Some 23,000 Soviet civilians were sent to Mauthausen.

SS-Hauptsturmführer Georg Bachmayer, deputy to Commandant Franz Ziereis in Mauthausen, is seen here inspecting a group of prisoners constructing the 'Russian camp'. Bachmayer's duties included overseeing granite production in the quarry. He also inspected the satellite camps and supervised the construction of the Ebensee concentration camp.

(**Above**) Prisoner labourers in the Stara Gradiška concentration camp. This camp was built in the independent state of Croatia and was established to house women and children of Serb, Jewish and Romani ethnicity. It was constructed by the Ustaše regime in 1941 by the use of forced labour.

(**Opposite, above**) In the roll-call square members of the orchestra can be seen here at the Janowska concentration camp performing in a circle around the conductor Yakub Mund. Pictured on the right in the light-coloured uniform is camp commandant *SS-Hauptsturmführer* Fritz Gebauer. The taller officer is camp commander *SS-Obersturmführer* Gustav Willhaus with his dachshund. The SS forced the orchestra to perform during selections and even 'commissioned' a special composition to be played on these occasions. It was entitled *Das Todestango* or 'The Tango of Death'.

(**Opposite, below**) Prisoners building the Dove-Elbe canal near Neuengamme in Germany. The *Kapos* overseeing the construction can be seen wearing white and black armbands.

Inmates can be seen here working outside in the Majdanek concentration camp. Following the invasion of Russia, on personal orders Himmler drafted a plan to build the concentration camp that was designed to house 25,000 PoWs. Construction began with 150 Jewish forced labourers from one of Globocnik's Lublin camps. Later the workforce included some 2,000 Russian PoWs who were treated brutally and had to survive extreme conditions including sleeping out in the open. Only 500 of them survived following a few months of hard labour.

A view of Majdanek concentration camp. In 1942 Majdanek was made into a secondary sorting and storage depot at the onset of Operation Reinhard, which was a secret operation to exterminate Polish Jews in Treblinka, Sobibor and Belzec. Although Majdanek was converted into its own killing centre in September 1942, the camp still operated as a multipurpose storage, labour and extermination facility.

Prisoners can be seen here working in the Majdanek concentration camp. Those classified as fit to work remained at the camp for forced labour. The majority, rejected as being unfit for work, were then sent to a gassing facility and murdered.

Prisoners can be seen here weaving baskets, possibly at one of the Jasenovac concentration camps. The camp was constructed in August 1941 in marshland at the confluence of the Sava and Una rivers near the village of Jasenovac in Yugoslavia. Many of the inmates, who were Serbs, were forced to work at the 'Brickworks' camp at Jasenovac and the five work farms.

Here prisoners can be seen breaking rocks at the Janowska concentration camp. In October 1941 the Germans established a concentration camp next to an SS-owned armaments factory that housed the forced labourers along with other prisoners. When the Germans liquidated the Lwów Ghetto, the ghetto's inhabitants that were fit for work were sent to the Janowska camp while the remainder were transported directly to the Belzec death camp for extermination in the summer of 1942.

A group of Jewish labourers are forced to have their photograph taken with a smiling guard at the Belzec concentration camp. Initially Jewish forced labour was sent to the camp in April 1940 for the construction of military defence facilities. The prisoners were also set to work by the SS to construct anti-tank ditches along the German-Soviet border, but this was abandoned during the onset of the invasion of Russia. Construction of the camp as a killing centre began in late 1941 and apart from some of the private companies brought in to assist in the building work, a great deal of slave labour was used.

An Ustaše guard stands next to a watch tower in the Jasenovac concentration camp.

Prisoners at the Jasenovac concentration camp are seen here during forced labour.

Those unfit for labour or too exhausted from overworking were killed. Here in this photograph taken near the Jasenovac concentration camp the Ustaše militia execute prisoners.

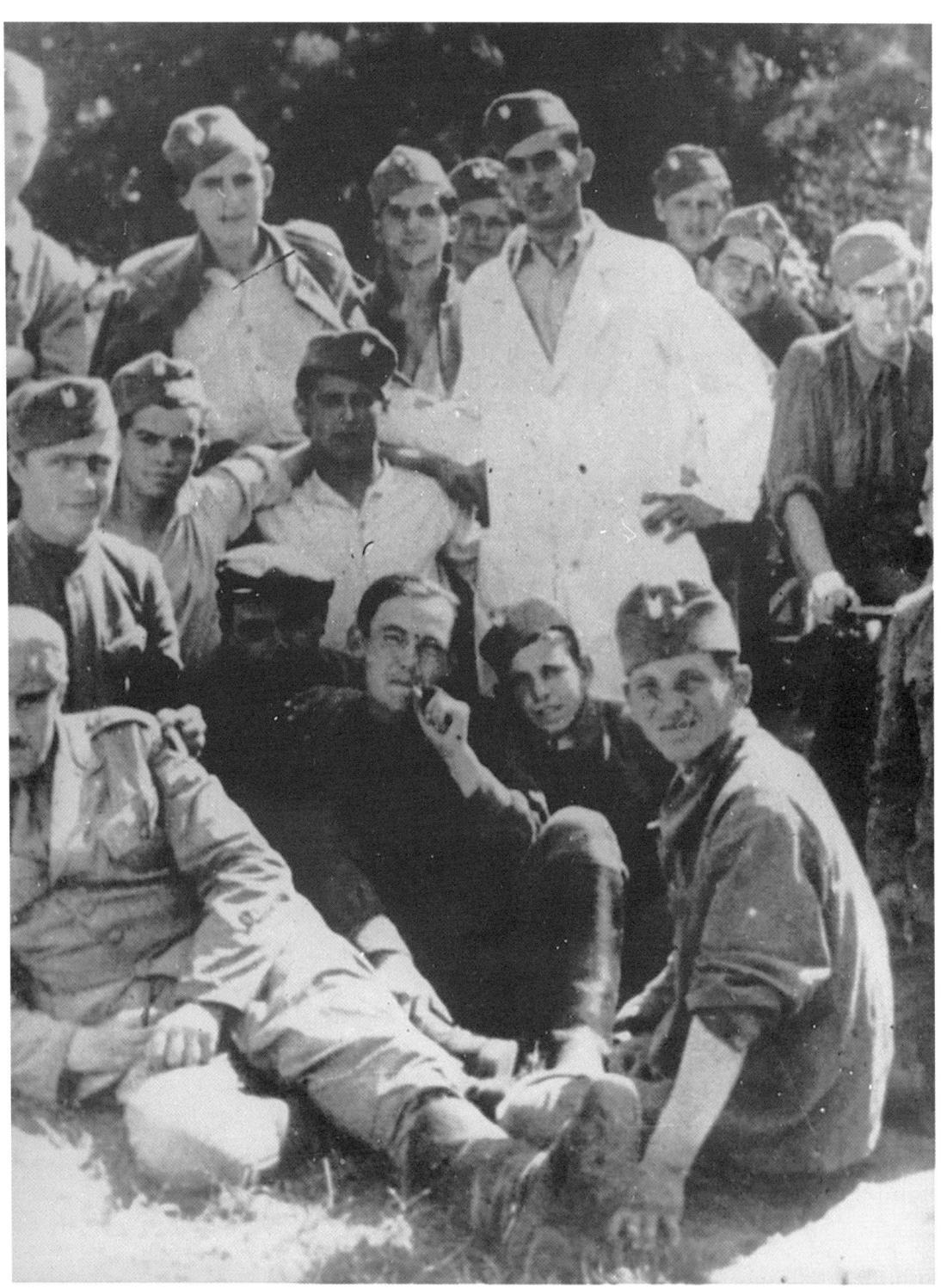
Ustaše guards following the murder of prisoners at the Jasenovac concentration camp.

An Ustaše guard poses here for the camera among all the dead who had been murdered near the Jasenovac concentration camp. Most executions of Jews at Jasenovac occurred prior to August 1942 and thereafter they were transported to Auschwitz. In general, Jews were initially sent to Jasenovac from all parts of Croatia after being gathered together in Zagreb and from Bosnia and Herzegovina.

Chapter Three

Extermination through Labour

The term 'Extermination through Labour' or *Vernichtung Durch Arbeit*' was adopted by the Nazis to describe forced labour throughout the concentration camp system. The SS authorities believed that if the inmates were held in inhumane conditions and worked to maximum extent they would suffer a high mortality rate. At the Wannsee Conference in January 1942, the Nazi leadership outlined the destruction of the Jewish race across the Reich and occupied territories. They planned to accelerate this destruction process by using the camps as a kind of natural extermination through hard labour. Notes for the minutes at Wannsee were taken down by Adolf Eichmann's secretary Ingeburg Werlemann and it was clear what the Nazis wanted to achieve:

> Under proper leadership, the Jews shall now in the course of the Final Solution be suitably brought to their work assignments in the East. Able-bodied Jews are to be led to these areas to build roads in large work columns separated by sex, during which a large part will undoubtedly drop out through a process of natural reduction. As it will undoubtedly represent the most robust portion, the possible final remainder will have to be handled appropriately, as it would constitute a group of naturally-selected individuals, and would form the seed of a new Jewish resistance.

Across the camp system 'Extermination through Labour' was principally carried out through what was characterized as 'slave work' and 'slave workers'. This was in stark contrast to the adoption of forced labour of foreign workers. For the Jews and other persons deemed racially inferior or a threat to the Reich, their labour would be physically demanding and work would include construction, farm and factory work and the arms industry, which was principally the most important area in which slave labour was required. Excessive working hours, often twelve hours per day with minimal nutrition, food rationing, poor medical care, lack of hygiene and disease ensured that life expectancy would be only a matter of weeks. This, together with various punishments and daily physical abuse, also hastened the death of many of the workers. The camp ritual, from the model of Dachau, was adopted across many of the camps and mirrored all aspects of camp life. From the admission and registration of prisoners, the housing conditions, the wearing of striped clothing and the long endless roll calls together with constant humiliation and harassment, all contributed to the wearing down of inmates both mentally and physically.

In some camps there were pointless tasks such as the heavy labour of moving rocks and stones from one location of the camp to another, all enforced by the SS to destroy what they referred as the 'mind and soul of the Jew'. Yet by 1942 there were many camps that used forced labour to benefit the German war economy. In order to get the maximum work output from an inmate the SS believed that excessive labour was key to success. Oswald Pohl, chief of the SS Main Economic and Administrative Office, was principally in charge of the employment of forced labour at concentration camps. On 30 April 1942 he sent out an order to his chain of command outlining the importance of the responsibility of the camp commandants in the achievement of maximum performance from slave labour:

> The camp commander alone is responsible for the use of manpower. This work must be exhausting in the true sense of the word in order to achieve maximum performance [...] There are no limits to working hours [...] Time-consuming walks and mid-day breaks only for the purpose of eating are prohibited [...] He [the camp commander] must connect clear technical knowledge in military and economic matters with sound and wise leadership of groups of people, which he should bring together to achieve a high performance potential.

Across the whole of the Reich and occupied territories the Nazis increased their use of slave labour. Albert Speer who served as Minister of Armaments and War Production was responsible for supplying weapons to the army. With Hitler's full agreement, he was given unrivalled power to ensure success across the armaments industry. This included the use of many hundreds of thousands of forced labourers. In order to achieve Speer's goal numerous camps were erected between 1942 and 1944 that solely used forced labour in order to boost the German war economy. However, life for those who were enslaved in these camps was hard and cruel. Camps like Kraków-Płaszów took only one month to construct using slave labour. The camp was divided into sections, but its primary function was forced labour. Its commandant *SS-Hauptsturmführer* Amon Göth was nicknamed 'the butcher of Płaszów'. He would often be seen screaming obscenities and beating and killing Jews. Prisoners recalled that 'he used to beat the prisoners with a completely expressionless, apathetic look on his face, as if the beatings were part of his daily routine.'

Other concentration camps also saw similar acts of brutality from their commandants and guards. At Ravensbrück women's concentration camp, which was primarily used for slave labour and medical experiments, its commandant *SS-Sturmbannführer* Fritz Suhren forced some prisoners to work in the camp brothel. Other prisoners 'volunteered' after being told that they would get special treatment or even release from the camp after six months, but nobody was ever released. Many of the prisoners were subjected to terrible acts of cruelty. Suhren's policy upon taking command in 1942 was to exterminate the prisoners through working them as hard as possible and feeding them as little as possible. He almost enjoyed meting out harsh and often brutal punishments for the slightest infractions of camp rules. He seemed to take great pride in the fact that his mere presence caused the female inmates to tremble with fear. While on work detail he regularly had the weak prisoners shot in front of the work force.

There were many violent commandants like the notorious *SS-Sturmbannführer* Otto Förschner of the Mittelbau-Dora concentration camp and the Dachau sub-camp of Kaufering. The Mittelbau-Dora camp was established in the late summer of 1943 as a sub-camp of Buchenwald and was constructed for slave labourers to work in the nearby mining tunnels in Kohnstein and in the manufacture of the V-2 rocket and V-1 flying bomb. Some 60,000 prisoners who were sent to the Mittelbau-Dora camp died.

In Estonia too there was the Vaivara concentration camp, which was the largest of the twenty-two concentration and labour camps established in the country. Some 20,000 Jewish prisoners were sent to the camp, mostly from the Vilna and Kovno ghettos but also from Latvia, Poland, Hungary and the Theresienstadt concentration camp. Many were forced to work and as a result died from illness, malnutrition or from their injuries incurred while working.

Across Germany as Speer continued to do whatever it took to increase armaments productivity, various production plants continued to employ forced labour. Audi was one of many companies that used forced labour on a massive scale. As a result some 4,500 deaths occurred at the Leitmeritz concentration camp. The aircraft manufacturer Heinkel used some 17,000 forced labourers and PoWs. The company mainly used inmates from Sachsenhausen concentration camp with several prisoners working on the Heinkel He 177 Greif (Griffin) bomber. Also in the Heinkel plant in Oranienburg forced labourers and prisoners were used extensively from the Sachsenhausen concentration camp and from the sub-camp of Ravensbrück.

SS-Reichsführer Heinrich Himmler and his entourage during an official visit to a Russian PoW camp in Minsk in August 1941.

Newly-arrived prisoners are assembled in the roll-call area at the Melk concentration camp. The camp's main purpose was to provide forced labour for various tunnelling projects in the surrounding hills. Work conditions were terrible and there were numerous deaths with prisoners being buried alive due to cave-ins. There were some 8,000 inmates contained in the camp and, strange though it may seem, the site was constructed within the confines of a large Wehrmacht garrison where both soldiers and civilians could see the inmates.

(**Below**) A view of the Ebensee concentration camp, a sub-camp of Mauthausen. The sub-camp was established by the SS purely to build tunnels for armaments storage near the town of Ebensee, Austria in 1943. Some 27,000 prisoners were housed in the camp – between 8,500 and 11,000 of them died.

(**Above**) The Kaufering IV concentration camp which was a sub-camp of Dachau concentration camp. There were eleven Kaufering sites built. It operated between June 1944 and April 1945. Jews were sent to Kaufering to construct three massive bunkers known as Weingut II, Diana II and Walnuss II. The bunkers were built purely for the construction of Messerschmitt Me 262 aircraft. Yet despite this being a late stage in the war when the labour force was desperately required, the Nazis still pursued their policy of 'Extermination through Labour' under which certain categories of prisoners were sometimes worked to death. The policy meant that many of the camp prisoners were forced to work under conditions of insufficient food, clothing, shelter or medical care which would directly and deliberately lead to their illness and death. Those that fell ill while in a work detail would be immediately killed or sent to the gas chambers if they did not die first.

(**Opposite, above**) Prisoners at forced labour on the assembly line of the Gustloff Werke II munitions plant in the Buchenwald concentration camp. The SS referred to this place as a 'war economy camp'. By early 1943 the Nazi government had intensively geared the concentration camp system towards aiding the war economy. As a result thousands of inmates went into operation in the spring of that year working for the Weimar weapons firm Wilhelm-Gustloff-Werke. Yet once again, despite the need for labour, the SS used their policy of 'Extermination through Labour' and as a result many thousands died in appalling conditions.

(**Opposite, below**) The Natzweiler-Struthof concentration camp. In late 1941, the SS established a camp in Natzweiler to mine a nearby granite quarry. Gradually other sub-camps were constructed, but the total number of prisoners still remained relatively small until late 1942. However, by 1943 the camp was expanded into south-west Germany and numerous small sub-camps were built.

A view of a section of the perimeter of the Natzweiler-Struthof concentration camp. At its peak the camp held some 19,000 prisoners until its evacuation in September 1944. During this period the inmates were subjected to torture, illness, injuries and exhaustion from being worked to death. More than 17,000 people died within the camp system.

A view of a barracks at the Plaszów concentration camp. This camp was divided into a number of sections comprising a satellite area for camp personnel, male prisoners, female prisoners, a subdivision just for Jews and non-Jews and a work facility. The camp's primary function was as a labour camp and it was a site of mass murders including annihilation through work. By 1943 the camp had expanded into the concentration camp system and was deemed a main camp. Thousands perished there through hard labour and mass shootings.

Two photographs showing the construction of the Gusen I concentration camp, which primarily housed Polish prisoners and a large contingent of Spanish Republicans, Soviet citizens and Italians. They initially worked in the nearby quarries under horrendous conditions. From 1943 the camp expanded to produce armaments and was designated as Gusen I. It was the largest sub-camp of Mauthausen and inmates that the SS wanted killed were actually sent to Gusen I for annihilation through work. In the eyes of the SS it was often in their interest to use whatever labour they could muster, even if it was just for a couple of days of hard labour.

A view of the entrance to the Arnstadt camp, a sub-camp of the Buchenwald concentration camp. The prisoners' tents are on the right and a small building for camp administrative matters is on the left. In the surrounding hills thousand of inmates worked on the construction of twenty-five tunnels. Many were overworked or brutally tortured during the construction – thousands of them perished.

Prisoners undertaking the construction of foundations for future barracks at the Stutthof concentration camp. During the course of the camp's existence between September 1939 and May 1945 some 110,000 people were deported there and as many as 65,000 of them perished.

Two inmates in a leather workshop in the Tărgu Jiu labour camp which housed Jews and communists. The site of the camp was at an old prison in the Romanian city of Tărgu Jiu. Many of those sent to the camp were subjected to forced labour.

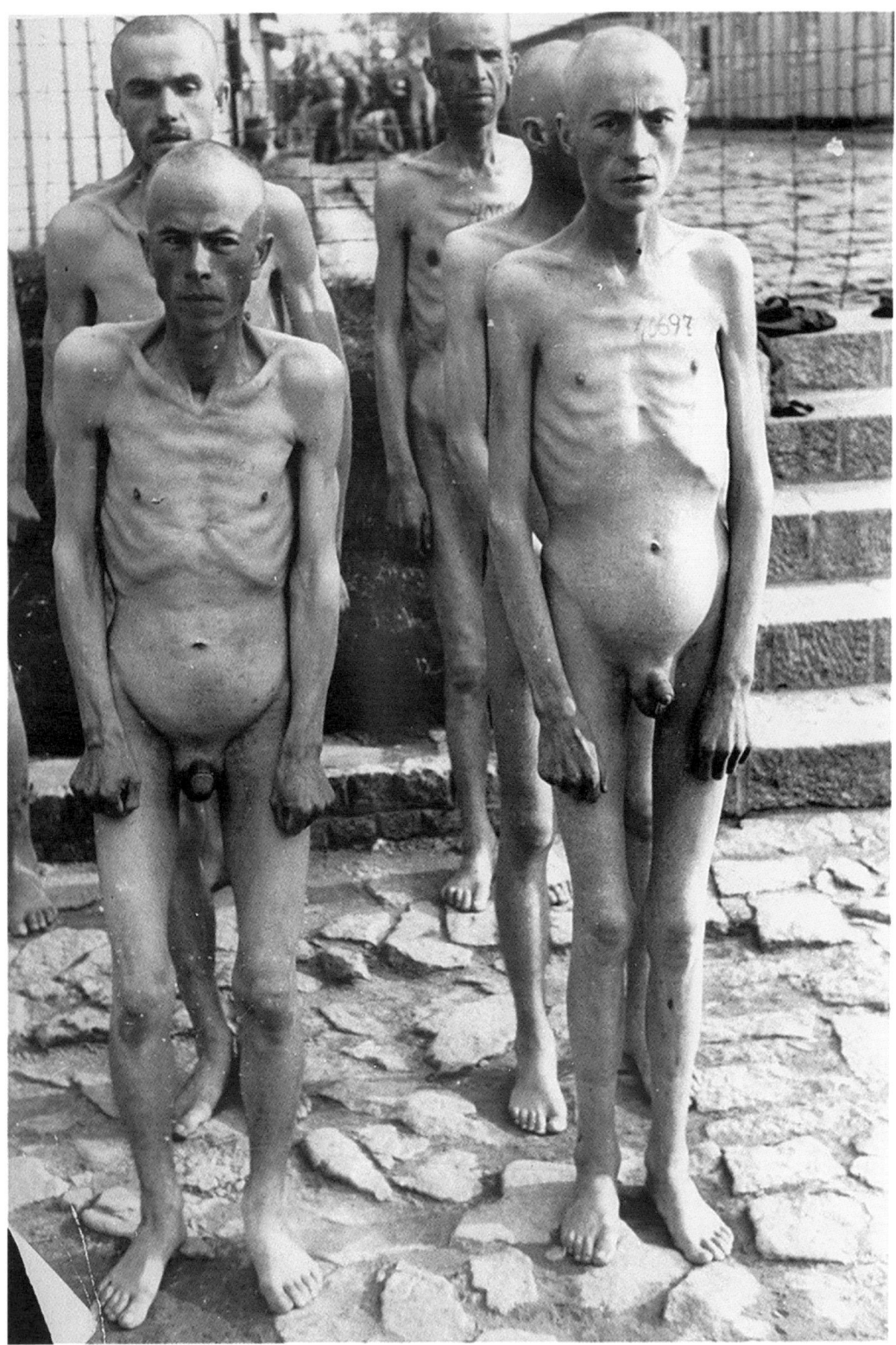

A group of naked Soviet PoWs, who in the autumn of 1944 were sent back to the Mauthausen main camp from the satellite camp of Melk, standing in line during a roll call.

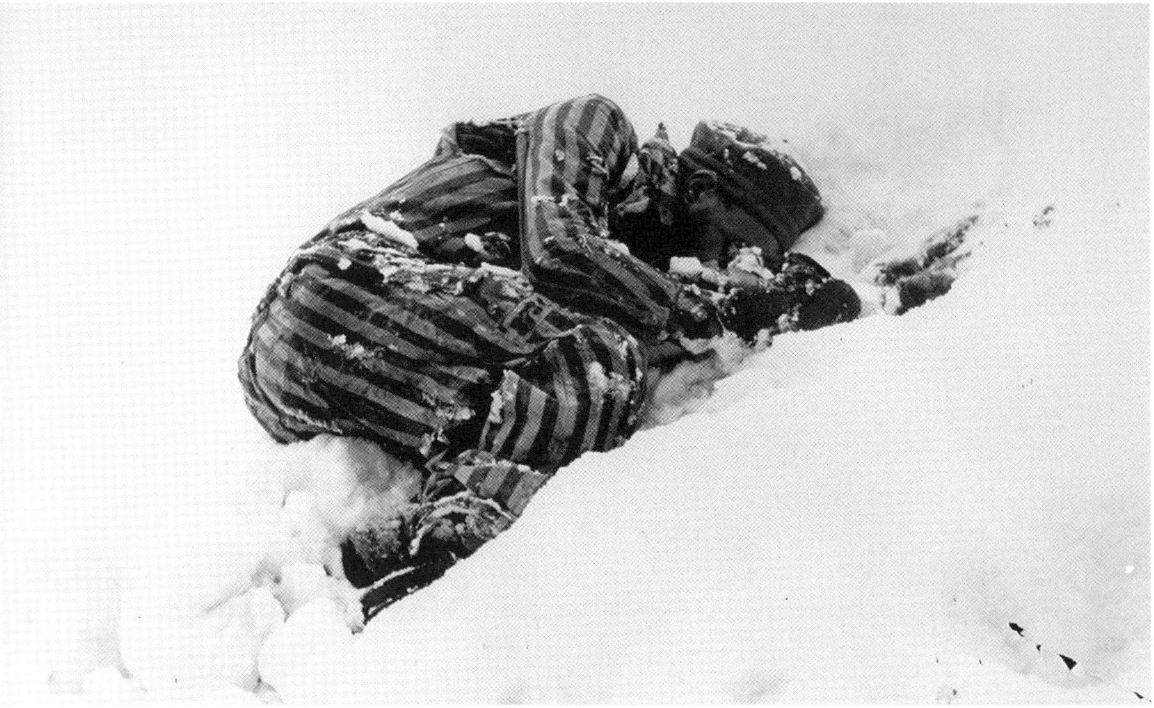

The frozen body of a Jewish prisoner lies in the snow after being beaten to death by the SS.

(**Below**) Seven photographs showing the rocket factory at Dora-Mittelbau, established in the late summer of 1943 as a sub-camp of Buchenwald concentration camp. The images show the camouflaged entrance to the underground rocket factory, tail fins of V-2 rockets on the tail section assembly line, the propulsion unit of a V-2 rocket, the testing department for the control section assembly of a V-2, the centre section or fuel section, the assembly line and the propulsion unit assembly section. By the summer of 1944 Mittelbau had become an independent camp with numerous sub-camps of its own. The death rate through work was around one in three of the 60,000 prisoners who were sent tthere. During the factory's operation the prisoners were subjected to extreme cruelty and starvation.

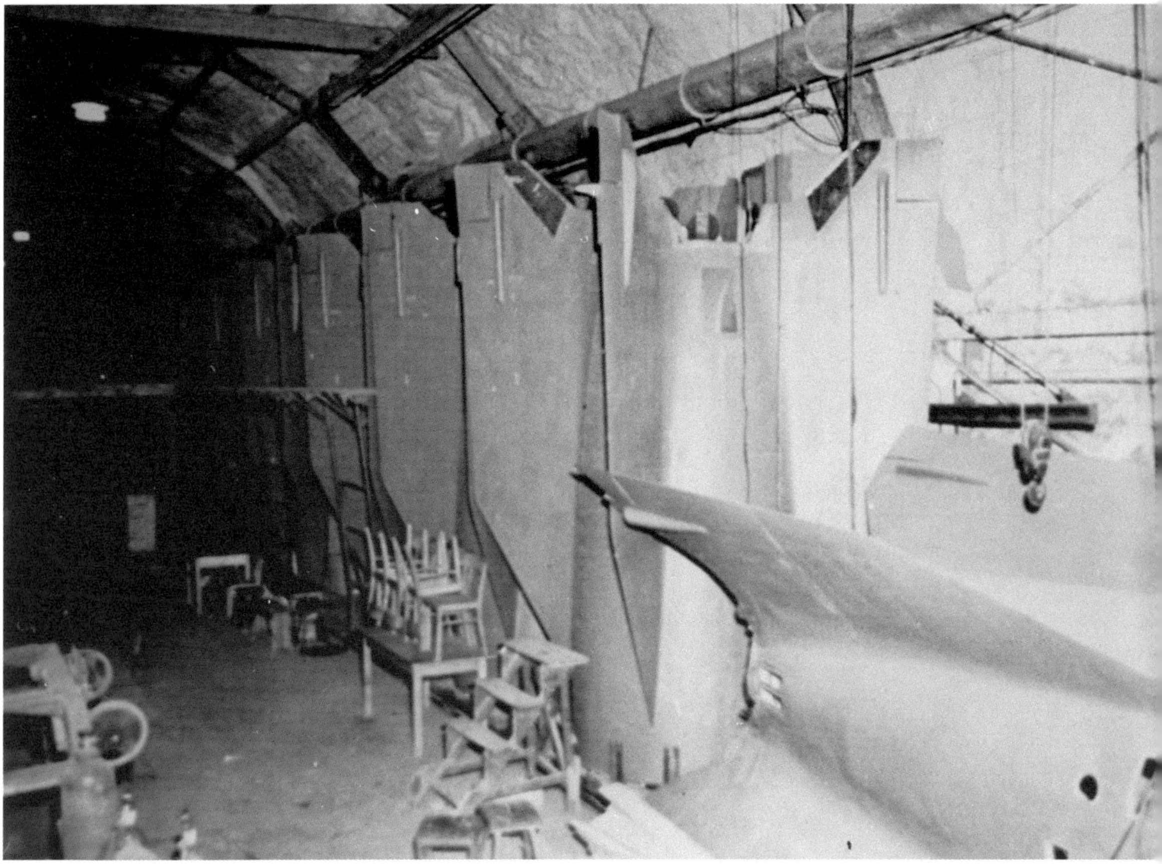

An internal view of an abandoned aircraft factory near Flossenbürg, where inmates of the nearby concentration camp were forced to work.

Chapter Four

Auschwitz

Overall the largest concentration camp built in Europe was Auschwitz. More than forty sub-camps were erected between 1942 and 1944. These sub-camps were built exclusively for various industrial plants and farms and a massive pool of slave labour was employed for their operation. In early 1941 Himmler had planned to transform what he saw was an old converted Polish barracks concentration camp into a massive complex. In March of that year when the first plans were drawn and approved for Birkenau, the *Reichsführer* intended to increase the Auschwitz camp population from the anticipated 10,000 inmates to 30,000. He made it clear that the massive increase in prisoner population was urgently required for labour availability, which was key to the progressive development of the region. Himmler envisaged that gangs of slave labour would be used to improve the dykes along the Sola and Vistula, and would also be put to work demolishing sites in the town for new building developments that were planned. In order to undertake these new developments, he said, all Jewish and Polish residents living around the camp were to be evicted and incarcerated in a camp in the neighbourhood of Auschwitz and used as unskilled construction workers. By evicting these people it would allow the town to be available for the factory staff of a new massive enterprise that Himmler was eager to see built in the local area, IG Farben.

Officials from this massive chemical cartel had come to Auschwitz with Himmler to finally decide whether a factory should be built in the area. For some time IG Farben had shown interest in the region around Auschwitz, and particularly welcomed using large numbers of skilled and unskilled construction workers from the concentration camps. It was estimated that between 8,000 and 12,000 men would be required to construct the factory, and with the *Reichsführer*'s new plans to increase the pool of prisoners at Auschwitz to 30,000 he had more than enough. By expanding Auschwitz he not only provided IG Farben with adequate amounts of slave labour, but could also commit 10,000 inmates to his planned agricultural estate as well.

The *Reichsführer*'s audacious plans for turning Auschwitz into a huge agricultural experimental centre were very much a fundamental part of his overall vision. Part of this plan involved using Auschwitz's sand and gravel pits for the German Earth and Stone Works enterprise. Himmler knew that the gravel pits would ensure the future growth of the camp, and for this reason Auschwitz had to be enlarged purely to house a permanent slave labour population.

Thousands of slave labourers, he said, would be used to enlarge the Auschwitz complex quickly and effectively. The very core of his vision was to Germanize Upper Silesia with agricultural workers. For this reason he planned to use Polish labour in large agricultural enterprises that would be put to work in building towns, villages, roads and drainage ditches. Auschwitz, he declared, was at the heart of this policy. A German settlement at Auschwitz would lay this foundation and from this model town of Germanization various villages would be erected. The *Reichsführer* had already envisaged that these Germanic villages would have a bell tower at the centre of the new settlements surrounded by a village hall, an inn, a school, a Hitler Youth home and kindergarten and buildings for the local farmers. He even intended to design villages comprising a number of settlements with the main village in the centre bordered by satellite villages. Concentrating these settlements together would ensure social cohesion and allow both the farmer and the land to prosper.

Himmler undoubtedly looked upon himself as the supreme architect of the German East and made it known that the areas now in the expanded Reich would soon be flourishing with German settlers. However, he was aware that it could not be done without the use of thousands of labourers including drafting in those already incarcerated in concentration camps and forced to work.

Plans were also drawn up and agreed for building factories including the production of armaments for the war effort. One factory that was approved was a huge synthetic rubber plant called Buna. The massive cartel company IG Farben had been given the highest priority. A site had been chosen for a factory about two miles away from Birkenau. Inmates from Auschwitz were to help construct it. Additional construction workers, also from Germany, would be brought in and accommodated in vacant homes in Auschwitz town. The town itself would be redeveloped and schools and hospitals built purely for the German workers.

In fact more than forty Auschwitz sub-camps would be erected between 1942 and 1944. Slave labour would be key to this development which comprised various German industrial plants and farms.

However, despite Himmler's audacious plans, by 1944 it was clear that the war in Russia was not going according to plan. Reverberations caused by a number of military setbacks and reverses on the Eastern Front were increasingly felt at Auschwitz, despite Germany's ardent determination to win the war. Plans for the building of the Auschwitz town had completely evaporated and the *Reichsführer*'s dreams of resettling millions of ethnic Germans in the East had been seriously curtailed. By the early summer of 1944 there was an ever-increasing need for more labour in the surrounding factories of Auschwitz. Strange though it may seem, in spite of this need for more labour it was estimated that only between 10 and 20 per cent of the people arriving on the ramps at Birkenau were selected for labour.

This selection process for new labour was undertaken very quickly. Often in double file the hand-picked labourers were sorted into males and females and the individual sexes were led into the camp, registered as prisoners and assigned the next numbers in the various series. They were then escorted to the Central Sauna brick building at the bottom of the camp. Its primary role was to carry out sanitary operations on all incoming able-bodied transports. Those that entered the building facility were undressed, had their hair cut, received a medical examination, were disinfected and then showered. They were given prisoner uniforms made of coarse grey-blue striped material and clogs which were standard issue in the concentration camp system and they were then marched to their allocated wooden stable-type barracks.

From here they were assigned their various types of labour and sorted into gangs. These tasks ranged from loading heavy materials to producing chemicals, mining, weapons and fuel or building. Others were put into special sorting gangs or 'clearing-up commandos'. Some men were rounded up and forced into the *Sonderkommandos* where they would have to work in the crematoria and assist in the incineration and disposal of corpses.

Slave labour at Auschwitz had been very lucrative for the SS and they looked upon the new arrivals in terms of increasing productivity. By the summer of 1944 there were already thousands of prisoners working in the satellite camps. Many of the arrivals selected for work detail often ended up working in the satellite camps. On 29 May, Hungarian inmates with A-series serial numbers were transferred to Monowitz, also known as Monowitz-Buna, Buna and Auschwitz III. Approximately 11,000 people were already working at the factory complex as slave labour. Gangs of labourers were sorted into work *Kommandos*, which ranged from several hundred prisoners to just a handful. Each *Kommando* had its own reference number and a name specifying the location or type of work.

Nearby other German industrial enterprises had built factories with their own sub-camps, such as Siemens-Schuckert's Bobrek complex and Krupp, all profiting from the use of slave labour. Again gangs were made up of work *Kommandos*. Their work details were often gruelling and under terrible conditions. The work was diverse and consisted of the transfer of construction materials, earthworks, the transport of narrow-gauge railway wagons filled with earth and the laying of power cables. Some inmates even worked as carpenters, roofers, painters and electricians.

After work the prisoners returned to the camp in their columns. Before 1944 there was a roll call, but because there were so many people in the camp this practice was abandoned. The harsh work, poor nutrition and general working conditions in the sub-camps resulted in many of the slave labourers being sent to Birkenau to be gassed.

It was not just at the Auschwitz satellite camps where newly selected labourers were sent to work. On 5 June 2,000 Hungarian labourers were sent to the Buchenwald concentration camp in Germany. Many of them worked in the female satellite camps in Mühlhausen, Gotha, Buttelstedt, Essen, Lippstadt, Weimar, Penig and numerous other sites. A week later on 13 June a shipment of approximately 2,000 were sent to Mauthausen and hundreds more were later transported. They were intended for tunnel construction at St Georgen and were mostly housed in camp Gusen II. The mortality rate of those among this group of prisoners was huge. Within months more than 2,100 of the 3,500 Hungarian Jewish prisoners at Gusen died there or were brought to Hartheim to be gassed.

Elsewhere across the Reich the need for labour continued to be desperate. Thousands of Jews including Hungarian Jews were diverted from being sent to Birkenau and were sent by rail to Vienna and Lower Austria for slave labour. Many more were later transported. Thousands of various nationalities, sometimes comprising whole families who would have met their fate at Auschwitz, were sent to Austria. They represented urgently needed manpower in factories and on farms. The deported families, mainly mothers, children and grandparents, had to work on farms, in construction companies, bread factories or oil refineries, all as forced labourers.

At Auschwitz, those deemed fit for labour were forced to work for more than eleven hours with scarcely any rest or proper tools, often working under brutal conditions. Even though the labour force was urgently required, the Nazis still pursued their policy of 'extermination through labour' under which certain categories of prisoners were sometimes worked to death. The policy meant that many of the camp prisoners were forced to work in conditions with insufficient food, clothing, shelter or medical care that would directly and deliberately lead to illness and death. Those that fell ill while in a work detail would be immediately sent to the gas chambers if they did not die first.

(**Opposite, above**) *SS-Brigadeführer* Richard Glücks stands carrying a briefcase with other SS men on an official visit to Gross-Rosen. Glücks was responsible for the forced labour of the camp inmates and was also the supervisor of the medical practices in the camps. It was Glücks who had recommended to *SS-Reichsführer* Heinrich Himmler on 21 February 1940 that Auschwitz should be chosen as a concentration camp. Glücks also accompanied Himmler and a number of directors of IG Farben on a visit to Auschwitz on 1 March 1941 when it was decided that the camp would be enlarged to hold as many as 30,000 prisoners. Furthermore, he discussed with Himmler an additional camp that should be constructed nearby and could be capable of housing some 100,000 PoWs. He also discussed building a factory in the Auschwitz area where camp prisoners could be placed at IG Farben's disposal. *(USHMM)*

(**Opposite, below**) The first of three photographs probably taken in May 1944 during the transportation of Hungarian Jews to Auschwitz. Jewish men and boys are seen here queuing along the ramp following a selection process for labour. For the SS at Birkenau age was a very important criterion during this process. Due to the high demand and the need for labour, healthy children as young as 14 years old were selected in the summer of 1944. *(Yad Vashem/The Archive of The State Museum Auschwitz-Birkenau in Oświęcim)*

Two photographs following the selection process of Hungarian males at Auschwitz-Birkenau. During May 1944, some 3,300 Hungarian Jews were arriving in the camp every day, but this figure rose as high as 4,300 on occasion. (*The Archive of The State Museum Auschwitz-Birkenau in Oświęcim*)

A third photograph following the selection process of Hungarian males at Auschwitz-Birkenau. On 20 May, a convoy came in carrying approximately 3,000 people, of whom only 1,000 were fit for labour. The following day two convoys arrived carrying 6,000 people, of whom only 2,000 were selected as being fit for labour. *(Yad Vashem/The Archive of The State Museum Auschwitz-Birkenau in Oświęcim)*

Men selected for labour are seen here more than likely being escorted to the camp's Central Sauna to be showered and re-clothed. The Central Camp Sauna, or 'bathhouse' as the SS named it, was purely designed for the mass disinfection and the extermination of insects in clothing. The primary role of this building was to carry out sanitary operations on all incoming able-bodied transports.
(The Archive of The State Museum Auschwitz-Birkenau in Oświęcim)

Those that entered the building facility would be undressed, have their hair cut, receive a medical examination, be disinfected and then showered. The SS regarded the building of the Central Sauna as the most efficient and practical method of reducing disease in the camp in order to work those who had been selected for labour. *(The Archive of The State Museum Auschwitz-Birkenau in Oświęcim)*

Men selected for labour are seen here after being sent to the camp's Central Sauna to be showered and re-clothed. These prisoners would be selected to perform various kinds of labour both inside and outside the camp boundaries. There were more than forty Auschwitz sub-camps surrounding Birkenau comprising various German industrial plants and farms. Thousands of labourers were sent out to work in these sub-camps. Those that fell ill or were too weak to perform their work detail were sent to the gas chambers and murdered. *(The Archive of The State Museum Auschwitz-Birkenau in Oświęcim)*

(**Above**) Jews from Subcarpathian Rus who had been selected for forced labour at Auschwitz-Birkenau are seen here waiting to be taken to another section of the camp. It was estimated that between 10 and 20 per cent of the people arriving on the ramps at Auschwitz-Birkenau were selected for labour.
(*The Archive of The State Museum Auschwitz-Birkenau in Oświęcim*)

(**Opposite**) Seven photographs showing Jews from Subcarpathian Rus who had been selected for forced labour at Auschwitz-Birkenau waiting to be taken to another section of the camp. After being sanitized at the camp's Central Sauna they were then marched to their allocated wooden stable-type barracks. From there they were given their labour tasks and put into gangs. These tasks ranged from loading heavy materials, producing chemicals, mining, weapons production and fuel or building. Others were put into special sorting gangs or 'clearing-up commandos'. Some men were rounded up and forced into the *Sonderkommandos* where they would have to work in the crematoria and assist in the incineration and corpse disposal. Many Jews chosen for work detail often ended up working in the satellite camps. On 29 May 1944, for instance, Hungarian inmates with A-series serial numbers were transferred to Monowitz, also known as Monowitz-Buna, Buna and Auschwitz III. Nearby other German industrial enterprises had built factories with their own sub-camps, such as Siemens-Schuckert's Bobrek complex and Krupp, all profiting from the use of slave labour. Again gangs were made up of work *Kommandos*. Their work details were demanding and carried out under terrible conditions. The work was diverse and consisted of the transfer of construction materials, earthworks, the transport of narrow-gauge railway wagons filled with earth and the laying of power cables. Some prisoners even worked as carpenters, roofers, painters or electricians. (*The Archive of The State Museum Auschwitz-Birkenau in Oświęcim*)

(**Below**) Female prisoners from Subcarpathian Rus transport who had been selected for forced labour march towards their barracks after disinfection, their heads shaved and a registration number tattooed on their left arms. (*The Archive of The State Museum Auschwitz-Birkenau in Oświęcim*)

Three photographs showing Jewish women from a Subcarpathian Rus transport marching towards their barracks in preparation for work detail. Many of the Hungarian women that were selected for work duties between May and July 1944 were made into *Kanadakommandos* (those who sorted the belongings of incoming prisoners) due to the high volume of transports arriving daily and the urgent requirement to process those that arrived. (*The Archive of The State Museum Auschwitz-Birkenau in Oświęcim*)

(**Below**) Female prisoners in the *Aufräumungskommandos* (order commandos) sort the confiscated property of a transport of Jews from Subcarpathian Rus at a warehouse in Auschwitz-Birkenau. *Kanada-kommandos* can be seen at the ramp clearing the possessions of the Jews. For the Hungarian operation in the summer of 1944 clearing-up commandos were enlarged to deal with the mass of people arriving daily. Prisoners working in the crematoria and in *Kanada* warehouses were to be brought out into the camp to assist in the sorting of Jewish property left at the ramp.
(*Yad Vashem/The Archive of The State Museum Auschwitz-Birkenau in Oświęcim*)

Prisoners in the *Aufräumungskommandos* (order commandos) and nicknamed *Kanadakommandos* sort through a mound of personal belongings confiscated from the Jews arriving from Subcarpathian Rus. The primary tasks of these special units were to assist in camp duties such as unloading Jews from trains with the assistance of the order commandos who were a group of recruited Jews used to unload the confiscated property of the transports. They were tasked with collecting transport possessions and sorting them for storage in the warehouse complex known as *Kanada*.
(Yad Vashem/The Archive of The State Museum Auschwitz-Birkenau in Oświęcim)

Female *Kanadakommandos* can be seen here sorting pots and pans from a recent transport of Jews.
(The Archive of The State Museum Auschwitz-Birkenau in Oświęcim)

Clothing from a Hungarian transport is seen here being unloaded from a vehicle. On 22 July 1944 210 male prisoners worked in *Kanada* I and 590 in *Kanada* II. *(USHMM/Yad Vashem)*

Here a cart is being hauled by *Kanadakommandos* containing numerous pots and pans. Note the volume of bags of possessions being unloaded from two transport vehicles at one of the *Kanada* warehouses. *(USHMM/Yad Vashem)*

Female *Kanadakommandos* seen here sorting through a pile of shoes.
(The Archive of The State Museum Auschwitz-Birkenau in Oświęcim)

Jewish people following a transport are seen resting near a pile of pots and pans.
(The Archive of The State Museum Auschwitz-Birkenau in Oświęcim)

The first of five photographs showing *Kanadakommandos* sorting possessions from transport vehicles. Prisoners who worked in *Kanada* were regarded as privileged. They were able to obtain extra rations and clothing from the possessions, items that could save their lives especially in the harsh conditions of the camp. Some of these prisoners also performed other duties in the camp. In order to speed the arrival of the Hungarian shipments some were drafted into duties on the ramp where they opened up the doors of the cattle cars when the new transports arrived. Here they helped the deportees to disembark and then, under strict supervision of the SS, they arranged the men and women into separate columns consisting of rows of five. They gathered the luggage scattered on the ramp and left in the cattle cars, loaded everything onto transport vehicles and transported the freight to the *Kanada* warehouses. The sorting began here: suitcases and bags were opened, and the objects were thoroughly searched and sorted by type. (*The Archive of The State Museum Auschwitz-Birkenau in Oświęcim*)

Two photographs showing female commandos sorting huge piles of possessions for the *Kanada* stores. By mid-July the majority of the warehouses were at their full capacity and as a result thousands of items of clothing, shoes, wicker baskets and kitchenware were often piled up outside.
(*The Archive of The State Museum Auschwitz-Birkenau in Oświęcim*)

Kanadakommandos sorting belongings from a shipment. From the end of May as more transports from Hungary arrived, hundreds of Hungarian Jewish women were assigned to preliminary work details in *Kanada* II, where in the summer of 1944 an average of 1,500-2,000 men and women performed work duties. *(USHMM/Yad Vashem)*

Chapter Five

Liberated

Throughout the war various concentration camps were shut down after either serving their purpose or they were closed for expanded newly-constructed camps in the area. Some camps operated for months and others for years. However, as German military reverses became more apparent camps were dismantled, evidence of their heinous crimes was concealed and those inmates who had not been murdered were walked on death marches to other camps, often to be worked to death.

As the Russians advanced through Poland in the summer of 1944 Soviet soldiers came across numerous concentration and work camps, factories, farms and other facilities erected by the German war machine. The majority had been abandoned in a hurry by the camp personnel, often leaving behind the main infrastructure. Although many thousands of slave labourers had been force-marched to other camps and facilities not yet overrun by the enemy, the liberating soldiers still found many inmates alive, some barely able to move or speak. The soldiers who arrived at these camps including small satellite installations were confronted by unimaginable conditions where evidence of half-burned corpses was found, and many of the inmates resembled skeletons due to the physical demands of forced labour and their lack of food.

What made it more unthinkable was that even as the Russians advanced within artillery range of some of the camps, guards were still mercilessly killing the prisoners or rounding them up to be marched to another facility. At Auschwitz, half of the 150,000 prisoners held in the camp were to be moved to concentration camps in the West. Camps like Buchenwald, Bergen-Belsen, Dachau, Flossenbürg, Gross-Rosen, Mauthausen, Natzweiler and Ravensbrück were all to receive the Auschwitz prisoners. Only some 7,000 inmates were left behind, with the majority being too weak and malnourished to move. At the Monowitz camp there were about 800 survivors.

As the Russians advanced further westwards in 1945, the Allies, on the Western Front, simultaneously advanced eastwards towards Germany. Camps such as Ohrdruf, Dachau, Buchenwald, Bergen-Belsen, Ravensbrück and Flossenbürg including its ninety-four sub-camps including the Nordhausen-Dora facility were liberated. The last camp to be liberated by American forces was Mauthausen concentration camp together with its forty-nine sub-camps which had been used for munitions factories, arms factories and plants for assembling the new

Messerschmitt Me 262 jet fighter. What they found at each of these sites was pure horror.

Although the Germans tried their best to conceal their crimes in the camps, the evidence found by the liberators when they arrived was overwhelming. The inmates who had survived being either almost worked or starved to death were later to speak of the inhumanities and reveal the truth of what they had suffered at the hands of the Nazis.

(**Below**) The bodies of prisoners lie stacked in a shed in the Ohrdruf concentration camp. The camp was established in November 1944 and included a separate labour camp directly controlled by the SS. By March 1945 some 20,000 inmates were housed in the camp mainly comprising Russians, Poles, Hungarian Jews, some French, Czechs, Italians, Belgians, Greeks, Yugoslavians and Germans. As the Allies advanced towards the camp the SS began evacuating Ohrdruf, forcing the inmates on death marches. In addition to those on the death marches an estimated 3,000 inmates died from exhaustion or were shot inside the camp.

(**Opposite, above**) Two emaciated survivors lie in a single bed in the newly-liberated Gusen concentration camp.

(**Opposite, below**) The bodies of prisoners killed in the Nordhausen concentration camp lie in mass graves dug by German civilians under orders from American troops.

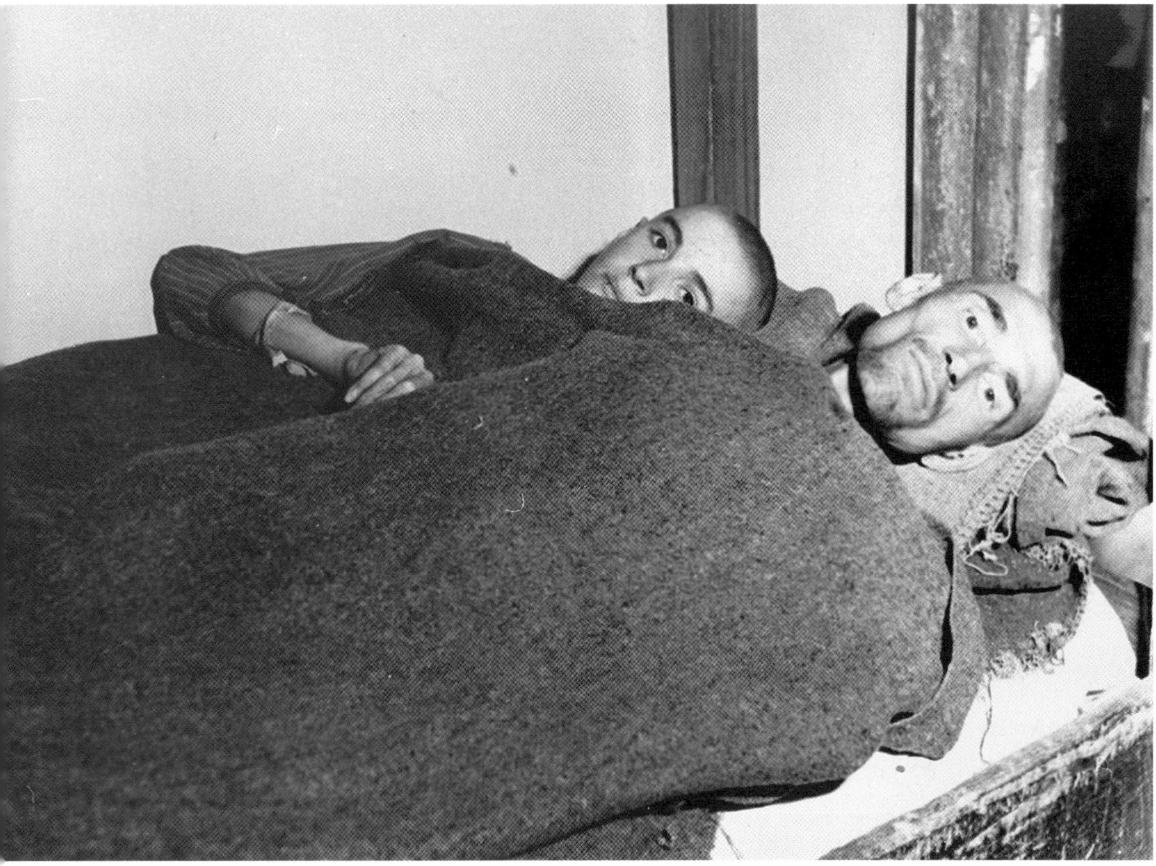

Survivors in Dachau cheer the arrival of US troops. More than 30,000 prisoners were liberated, mainly Jews and political prisoners. In the surrounding area the sub-camps were liberated as well.

A survivor in Dachau on the day of liberation, 29 April 1945.

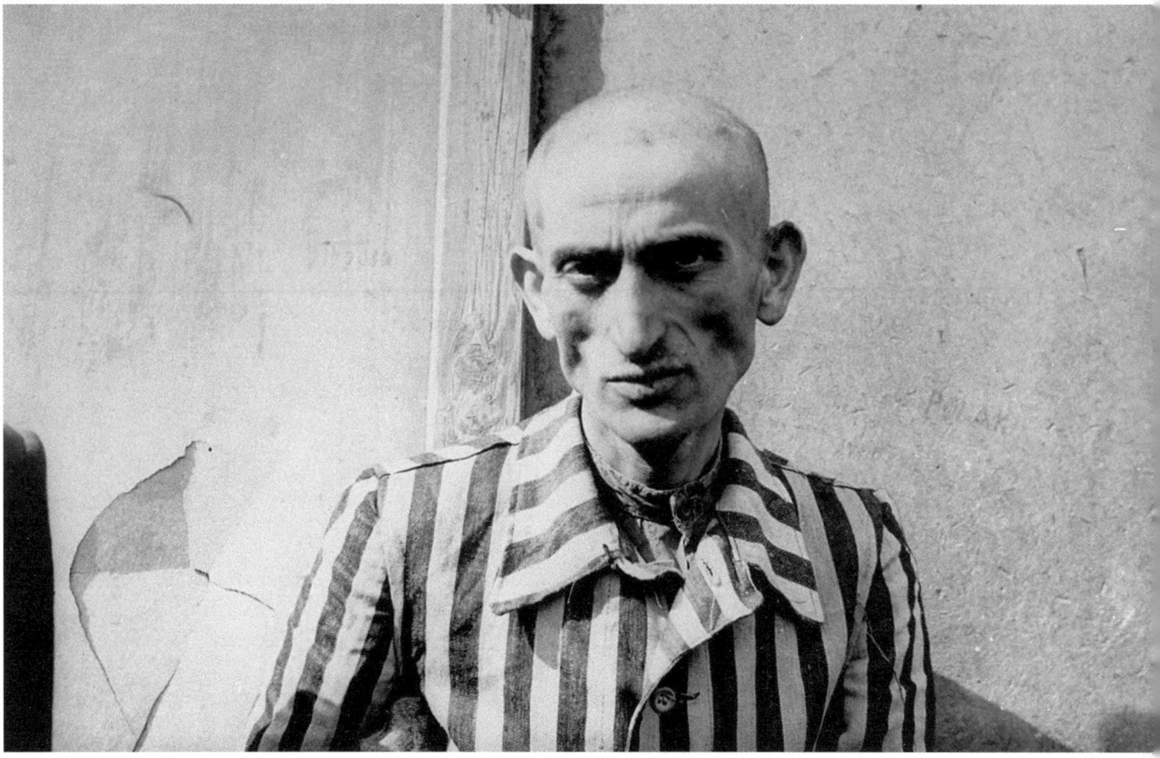

Corpses lying beside the rail spur that served the Kaufering IV concentration camp. Kaufering was a system of eleven sub-camps of the Dachau concentration camp which operated between 18 June 1944 and 27 April 1945.

Survivors in a barrack in the Kaufering IV concentration camp. As the Allied troops approached, the Germans were going to massacre everyone in the camp before liberation. However, hundreds were evacuated from Kaufering and arrived at the Buchberg labour camp on 29 April 1945.

Survivors in the Ampfing concentration camp standing outside the camp infirmary.

Survivors in the Ampfing concentration camp standing on a camp street outside their barracks.

Survivors in a barracks in the Ampfing concentration camp.

Survivors carrying water in the Ampfing concentration camp which was a sub-camp of Dachau.

A group of emaciated survivors in the infirmary barracks for Jewish prisoners in the Ebensee concentration camp. The camp was liberated by the US Third Army.

Survivors waving to American liberators from their bunks in the infirmary barracks for Jewish prisoners in the Ebensee concentration camp.

Survivors looking out from the upper tier of a bunk in the infirmary barracks for Jewish prisoners in the Ebensee concentration camp.

Corpses in the Wöbbelin concentration camp, liberated on 2 May 1945 by the US 8th Infantry Division and the 82nd Airborne Division. They found some 1,000 inmates dead in the camp.

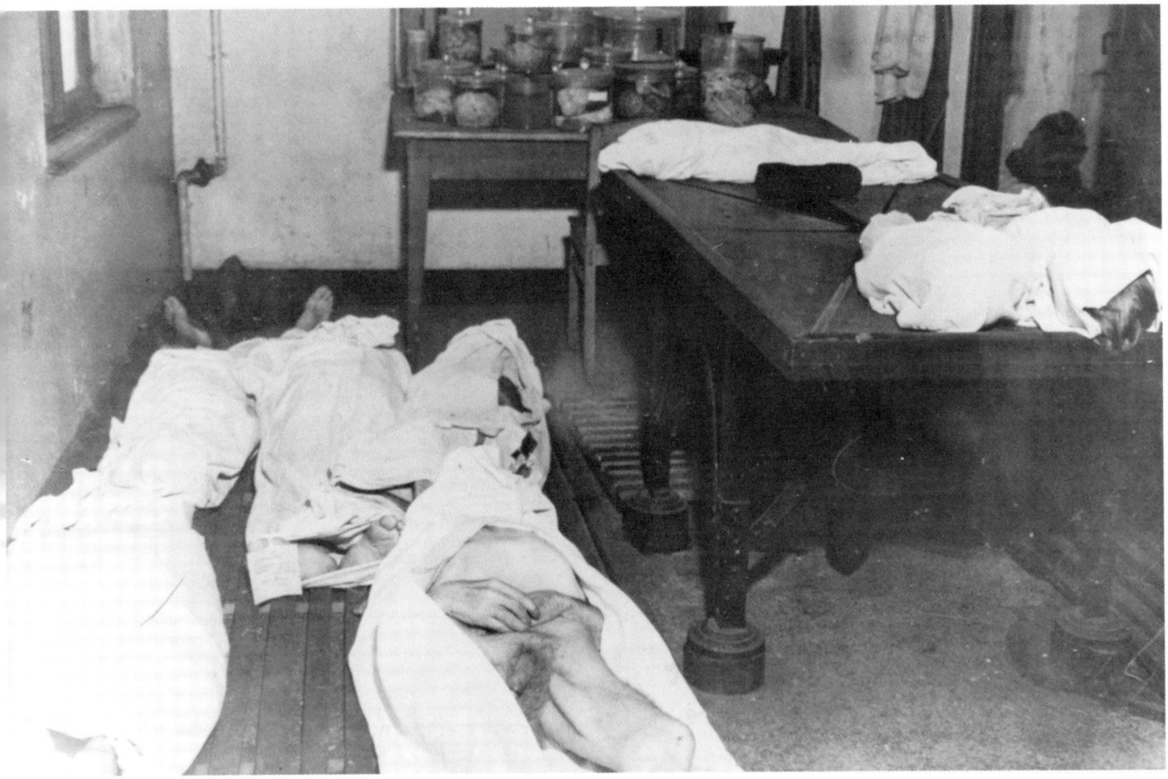

Sheets covering the bodies of slave labourers found in a room in the Dortmund PoW camp. On the table are the bodies of four young children.

A liberated section of Bergen-Belsen concentration camp. In April 1943, part of the camp was taken over by the SS Main Economic and Administrative Office (*SS-Wirtschafts-Verwaltungshauptamt* or WVHA) and became part of the concentration camp system. In June 1943 it became a holding camp.

(**Opposite**) Commandant of Bergen-Belsen Josef Kramer shackled following the liberation of the camp. Kramer was an *SS-Hauptsturmführer* who had been transferred from Auschwitz-Birkenau as camp commander to Bergen-Belsen. The camp was opened in April 1943 for 500 inmates and the families incarcerated there were able to stay together and were allowed to wear their own clothes. By the summer of 1944 the camp was overcrowded with Hungarian Jews and conditions steadily worsened. The commandant, *SS-Sturmbannführer* Adolf Haas, had been blamed for neglecting the camp and it was decided that he was to be relieved of his command. On 1 December Kramer was transferred to Belsen and he arrived from Auschwitz with a large number of prisoners who had been part of the evacuation order. The march had been horrific with long columns of prisoners trudging many miles through rain and cold. Hundreds had dropped through sheer exhaustion and died by the roadside, while others too weak to go on were shot by the guards. Kramer was utterly callous about the conditions on the march and made little effort to check that the prisoners had adequate supplies or shelter. Himmler hoped that Kramer's brutal approach would dispel SS rumours that the camp was for the 'so-called pampered Jews'. As newly-appointed commandant, Kramer was callous and heartless. Even though sanitary conditions were far worse than at Auschwitz and the prisoner barracks were 'totally run down', he did little to decrease the death rate. The overcrowding was also dreadful and made worse by the arrival of the first batch of Auschwitz evacuees. (*USHMM*)

(**Above**) The liberated women's barracks in Bergen-Belsen. Although certain camp inmates had work duties, the camp was not a labour camp; its primary function was as a holding camp. However, some inmates had been forced labourers and came to Belsen from camps such as Flossenbürg, Gross-Rosen, Ravensbrück, Neuengamme, Mauthausen and Buchenwald concentration camps as well as various sub-camps and labour camps. Many inmates were to perish through disease and illness.

Barracks in Bergen-Belsen concentration camp. By the end of July 1944 there were some 7,000 prisoners interned in the Bergen-Belsen camp complex. Within six months that figure had doubled and by February 1945 there were 22,000 inmates. Thousands of prisoners evacuated from other camps continued to arrive between February and April 1945. As a result the camp population increased considerably despite the high death rate.

Appendix I

List of Concentration Camps and Sub-Camps

The majority of these camps were either dismantled or destroyed by the German authorities, often within weeks of their operation.

Germany
Bergen-Belsen
   (probably 2 sub-camps, location is not known)
Börgermoor
   (no sub-camp known)
Buchenwald
   (174 sub-camps)
Buchenwald/Dora-
   Mittelbau
Abterode
Adorf
Allendorf
Altenburg
Annaburg
Arnstadt
Arolsen
Artern
Ascherleben
Baalberg
Bad Berja
Bad Godesberg
Bad Handersheim
Bad Salzungen
Ballenstadt
Baubrigade I-X
Bensberg
Berga/Elster
Berlstedt
Bernburg
Billroda
Birkhan-Motzlich

Bischofferode
Blankenburg
Blankenheim
Bleicherode
Bochum I
Bochum II
Bodtenberg
Böhlen
Braunschweig
Buttelstedt
Clus
Coblence: 'rebstock'
Colditz (Hasag)
Cologne I
Cologne II
Cologne III
Crawinkel
Dernau
Dessau I
Dessau II
Dornburg
Dortmund
Duderstadt
Düsseldorf I
Düsseldorf II
Düsseldorf III
Eisenach
Ellrich
Elsnig
Eschenhausen
Escherhausen
Essen I

Essen II
Flossenbürg
Freiheit-Osterode
Gandersheim
Gelsenkirchen
Giessen
Gleina
Goslar
Göttingen
Grasleben
Grosswerther
Günzerode
Hadmersleben
Halberstadt
Halberstadt-Zwieberge
Hardehausen
Harzungen
Hasserode
Herzberg/Elster
Hessich-Lichtenau
Hinzert
Hohlstedt
Holzen
Ilfeld
Ilsenburg
Jena
Kassel
Kelbra
Klein bischofferode
Klein bodungen
Klein niedergerba
Kleinnoshersleben

113

Köln fordwerke	Sangerhausen	Ampersmoching
Köln hansestadt	Schlieben (Hasag)	Asbach-Baumenheim
Köln westwagen	Schönau	Aufkrich-Kaufbeuren
Kranichfeld	Schönbeck (Hasag)	Augsburg
Langensalsa	Schwalbe V	Augsburg-Haunstetten
Langenstein	Schwerte	Augsburg-Pfersee
Lauenberg 'Laura'	Sennelager	Augustenfeld-Pollnhof
Lehensten 'Laura'	Sollstedt	Bad Ischl
Leimbach	Sömmerda	Bad Ischl Saint Wolfgang
Leipzig (Hasag)	Sonneberg	Bad Tolz
Leipzig Lindenthal	Stassfurt	Bad Bayernsoien
Leipzig Markkleeberg	Stutzpunkt Sauerland 1	Baubrigade XIII
Leipzig Schönauer	Suhl	Bayrishezell
Leopoldshall	Tannenwald	Bichl
Lippstadt	Tanndora	Birgsau-Oberstdorf
Lohausen	Taucha (Hasag)	Blainach
Lützkendorf	Thekla (Erla-Werke)	Brunigsau
Magdeburg I	Tonndorf	Burgau
Magdeburg II	Torgau	Burghausen
Markkleeberg	Trautenstein	Burgkirchen
Merseburg	Troglitz (Brabag)	Donauworth
Meuselwitz	Unna	Durach-Kottern
Muhlhausen 'Martha'	Walkenried-Wolfleben	Eching
Neustadt	Wansleben	Ellwagen
Niederorshel	Wansleben 'Biber II'	Emmerting-Gendorf
Niedersachswerfen	Wansleben 'Wilhelm'	Eschelbach
Nordhausen I	Weimar	Feistenau
Nordhausen II	Weimar-Fischtenhain	Feldafing
Nordhausen III	Werferlingen	Fischbachau
Nuxei	Wernigerode	Fischen
Oberndorf	Westeregeln	Fischhorn/Bruck
Ohrdruf	Wewelsburg	Freising
Oschersleben 'Ago'	Wickerode	Friedolfing
Osterhagen	Wieda	Friedrischaffen
Osterode	Witten-Annen	Fulpmes
Penig (Gehrt)	Wöbbelin	Fussen-Plansee
Plomnitz	Wolfen	Gablingen
Quedlinburg I	Wuppertal	Garmisch-Partenkirchen
Quedlinburg II	Zeitz 'Willy'	Germering-Neuaubing
Raguhn	Zella Mehlis	Gmund
Rehmsdorf 'Willy'	Zorbig	Grimolsried-Mitteneuf-Nach
Römhild	**Dachau** (123 sub-camps)	
Rossla	Aibing	Halfing
Rothenburg	Allach	Hallein
Rottleberode	Allach/Karsfeld/Moosach	Hausham-Vordereckard
Saalfeld-Örtelsbruch	Allach-Rothwaige	Heidenhaim
Salza-Thuringe	Allersdorf-Liebhof	Heppenhaim

Horgau-Pfersee
Hurlach
Ingoldstadt
Innsbruck
Itter
Karlsfeld
Kaufbeuren
Kaufering
Kaufering Erpfting
Kempten-Kotern
Königssee
Krucklhalm
Landsberg
Landshut-Bayern
Lauingen
Lechfeld
Liebhof
Lind
Lochau
Lochhausen
Lohof
Markt Schwabben
Mettenheim
Mittel-Neufnach
Moosach
Moschendorf-Hof
Muldorf
Muldorf Ampfing-
 Waldlager V and VI
München
München Friedman
München Riem
München Schwabing
München Sendling
Neuburg Donau
Neufahrn
Neustift
Nuremberg
Oberdorf
Oberföhring
Obertaufkirchen
Ottobrunn
Ötztal
Passau
Puchheim
Radolfzell
Riederloh

Rohrdorf-Thansau
Rosenheim
Rothschwaige-
 Augustenfeld
Salzburg
Salzweg
Sandhoffen
Saulgau
Schlachters-Sigmarszell
Schleissheim
Schwabbeg
Schwabmuünchen
Seehausen-Uffing
Spitzingsee
St. Gilden/Wolgansee
St. Lambrecht
Steinhöring
Stephanskirchen
Strobl
Sudelfeld
Traustein
Trotsberg
Trutskirch-Tutzing
Turkenfald
Turkheim
Überlingen
Ulm
Unterschleissheim
Utting
Valepp
Vulpmes
Weidach
Weilheim
Weissensee
Wicking
Wolfratshausen
Wolfratshausen Gelting
Wurach-Wolhof
Zangberg

Altenhammer
Annaberg
Ansbach
Aue (Sachsen)
Bayreuth
Beneschau
Bozicany

Brüx
Chemnitz
Dresden
Eisenberg
Erbendorf
Falkenau
Flöha
Forrenbach
Freiberg
Ganacker
Giebelstadt
Grafenreuth
Graslitz
Gröditz
Gundelsdorf
Hainichen
Happurg
Heidenau
Helmbrechts
Hersbruck
Hertine
Hof
Hohenstein-Ernstthal
Holleischen
Holyson
Hradischko
Hubmersberg-Hohenstadt
Janowitz
Jezeri
Johanngeorgenstadt
Jungfern-Breschan
Kaaden-Kadan
Kamenicky-Senow
Kirchham
Knellendorf
Königstein
Krondorf
Leitmeritz
Lengenfeld
Lobositz
Mehltheuer
Meissen
Mittweida
Moickethal-Zatschke
Moschendorf
Mülsen-St. Michel
Münchberg

Neu Rohlau
Nossen
Nuremberg
Obertraubling
Oederan
Olbramowitz
Pilsen
Plattling
Plauen
Pocking
Porschdorf
Poschetzau
Pottenstein
Praha
Rabstein
Rathen
Rathmanndorf
Regensburg
Reuth
Rochlitz
Saal/Donau
Schlackenwerth
Schönheide
Seifhennersdorf
Siegmar-Schönau
St. Georgenthal
St. Ötzen
Stein-Schönau
Stulln
Theresienstadt
Venusberg
Wilischthal
Witten-Annen
Wolkenburg
Würzburg
Zatschke
Zschachwitz
Zschopau
Zwickau
Zwodau

Ahlem-Hannover
Altegarde-Elbe
Altgarga
Aumund
Aurich-Engerhafe
Bad Sassendorf

Barkhausen
Barskamp
Baubrigade I, II, V and XI
Beendorf-Helmstedt
Bergstedt
Blumenthal
Boizenburg
Braunschweig
Bremen-Farbe
Bremen-Osterort-Reisport
Bremen-Schützenhof
Bremen-Vegesack-
    Aumund
Bremen-Weser
Brink-Hannover
Brunswick-Busing
Dalum
Dreutte
Engerhafe
Fallersleben-Laagberg
Farge
Fidelstedt
Finkenwerder
Fuhlsbüttel
Geilenberg
Glassau-bei-Sarau
Goslar
Gross-Fullen
Gross-Hesepe
Hamburg
Hausberge-Porta
Helmstadt
Hidelsheim
Horneburg
Howachts-Lütjenburg
Kaltenkirch-Heinkaten
Kiel
Laasberg
Ladelund
Langenhagen-Hannover
Langenhorn-Hamburg
Lengerich
Lerbeck
Limmer-Hannover
Linden
Lübberstadt
Ludwigslust

Lütjenburg
Meppen
Minden
Misburg-Hannover
Mölln
Neesen
Neugraben
Neuhof
Neuland-Bremen
Neunkirchen
Neustadt
Nutzen
Ohldorf
Osnabrück
Osterort
Poppenbüttel-Sasen
Porta-Westfalica
Salzgitter
Salzwedel
Sandbostel
Sasel
Schandelah
Schützenhof-Bremen
Schwessing-Husum
Sollstadt
Spaldingstrasse
Steinwerder
Stöcken-Hannover
Stuklenwert
Tiefstak
Uelzen
Veersen
Vegesack-Aumun-Bremen
Veleen
Verden-Aller
Wandsbeck
Watenstedt-Drütte-
    Salzgitter
Wedel
Wilhemsburg-Hamburg
Wilhemshaven
Wittenberge
Wolfsburg
Wöbbelin-Ludwigslust
Dieburg (no sub-camp known)

Esterwegen
 (1 sub-camp)
Flossenbürg
 (94 sub-camps)
Gundelsheim
 (no sub-camp known)
Neuengamme
 (96 sub-camps)
Papenburg
 (no sub-camp known)
Ravensbrück
 (31 sub-camps)
Abteroda
Ansbach
Barth/Ostee
Belzig
Berlin-Oberschöneweide
Berlin-Schönefeld
Borkheide
Bruckentin
Comthurey
Dabelow
Eberswalde
Feldberg
Fürstenberg
Hennigsdorf
Herzebrück
Hohenlychen
Karlshagen
Klützow-Stargard
Köningsberg-Neumark
Malchow
Neubrandenburg
Neustadt/Glene
Peenemünde
Prenzlau
Rechlin
Retzow
Rostock-Marienhe
Schwarzenforst
Stargard
Steinhöring
Uckermark
Velten
Sachsenhausen
 (44 sub-camps)
 Babelsberg

Bad Saarow
Baubrigade I, II, III, IV, V,
 VI, VII, VIII, IX, X, XI
 and XII
Beerfelde
Berga
Berlin
Falkensee
Helensee (Demag)
Hennigsdorf (AEG)
Köpenick
Lichtenrade
Lichterfelde
Reinickendorf (Argus)
Siemens Stadt
Tegel
Wilmersdorf

Biesenthal
Bornicke
Brandenburg/Havel
Dammsmühle-Schönwalde
Debno-Neudamm
Döberitz
Drogen-Niedorf
Falkenhagen-Fürstenwalde
Falkensee
Friesoythe/Cloppenburg
Genshagen
Glau-Trebbin
Gross-Rosen
Heinkel
Hohenlychen
Karlsruhe
Kleinmachnow
Klinker
Kolpin
Königs Wusterhausen
Küstrin
Lieberose
Lubben
Muggelheim
Neubrandenburg
 (Hamburg)
Neustrelitz
Niederhagen
Oranienburg

Politz
Prettin
Rathenow
Ravensbrück (until 1939)
Riga
Senftenberg/Schwarzweide
Storkow
Stuttgart
Treuenbrietzen
Werde
Wewelsburg
Wittenberg (Arado)
Sachsenburg
 (no sub-camp known)

Austria
Mauthausen
 (49 sub-camps)
Aflenz
Redl-Zipf (code-name
 Schlier)
Amstetten (2 camps:
 male and female)
Bachmanning
Bretstein
Diepoldsau
Ebelsberg
Ebensee
Eisenerz
Enns
Floridsdorf
Grein
Grossraming
Gunskirchen
Gusen I, II, III
Hinterbrühl
Hirtenberg
Klagenfurt
Kleinmünchen
Leibnitz
Lenzing
LindLinz I, II, III
Loibl – Pass Nord
Loibl – Pass Süd
 (ex-Yugoslavia)
Melk
Mittersill
Passau I – Waldwerke

Passau II
Peggau
St. Agyd
St. Lambrecht
St. Valentin
Steyr
Ternberg
Vöcklabrück/Wagrain
Wels
Wien Afa-Werke
Wien Saurer-Werke
Wien-Schwechat
Wien Schönbrunn
Wiener Neudorf
Wiener Neustadt

Czechoslovakia
Theresienstadt
Alhostice
Bohušovice
Kopisti
Litoměřice
Litoměřice-Radobylberg
Lovosice
Neštěmice
Stí
Terezín
Kratzau/Chrastava
  (sub-camp of **Gross-Rosen – Rogožnica**, Poland)

Belgium
Breendonk (no sub-camp known)

Czechoslovakia
Theresienstadt
  (9 sub-camps)

Estonia
Vaivara

Finland
Kangasjärvi
Kõveri

France
Argelès
Aurigny
Brens
Drancy Gurs
Le Vernet
Les Milles

Germany
Natzweiler-Struthof
  (70 sub-camps)
Asbach
Auerbach-Bensheim
Bad-Oppenau
Baden-Baden
Balingen
Bisingen
Dautmergen
Dormettingen
Erzingen
Frommern
Scherzingen
Schomberg
Wüste
Zepfenhan

Bernhausen
Bingau
Bischofsheim
Calw
Cernay
Cochem
Cochem Treis
Colmar
Darmstadt
Daudenzell
Dautmergen
Donauwiese
Echterdingen
Ellwangen
Ensingen
Frankfurt am Main
Frommern
Geisenheim
Geislingen
Goben
Gross-Sachsenheim
Güttenbach
Hailfingen
Haslach
Heilbronn
Heppenheim
Hessenthal
IffezheimIffezheim – Baden
  Oos-Sandweiller
Kaisheim
Kochendorf
Leonberg
Longwy-Thiel
Mannheim
Metz
Mosbach
Neckarelz I and II
Neckarelz Bad Rappenau
Neckargartach-Heilbronn
Neckargerach
Neckargerach
  Unterschwarsach
Neunkirchen
Oberehnheim-Obernai
Obrigheim
Peltre
Plattenwald
Rothau
Saint-Die
Sainte Marie aux Mines
Sandweier
Sanhofen
Schirmeck
Schönberg
Schörzingen
Schwabisch-Hall
Spaichingen
Tailfingen
Urbes Wesserling
Vaihingen-Enz
Vaihingen/Unterriexingen
Wasserralfingen
Weckrieden
Wasserling
Zuffenhausen
Noé
Récébédou
Rieucros
Rivesaltes

Suresnes
Thil

North Africa
Abadla
Ain el-Ourak
Béchar
Berguent
Bogari
Bouarfa
Djelfa
Kénadsa
Méridja
Missour
Tendrara

Holland
Amersfoort
Ommen
Vught (12 sub-camps)
Amhem
Breda
Eindhoven
Gilze en Rijen
's-Gravenhage (The Hague)
Haaren par Tilburg
Leeuwarden
Moerdijk
Rozendaal
Sint-Michielsgestel
Valkenburg par Leiden
Venlo
Westerbork (transit camp)

Italy
Bolzano
Fossoli
Risiera di San Sabba (no sub-camp known)

Latvia
Dundaga
Eleje-Meitenes
Jungfernhof
Lenta
Riga
Riga-Kaiserwald
Spilve

Lithuania
Aleksotaskowno
Kaunas
Palemonas
Pravieniškės
Volary

Norway
Bærum
Berg
Bredtvet
Falstadt
Tromsdalen
Ulven

Poland
Auschwitz-Birkenau (extermination camp – 51 sub-camps)
Altdorf/Stara Wieś
Althammer/Stara Kuźnia
Babice
Bauzug
Beruna
Bismarckhütte/Chorzów Batory
Blechhammer/Sławięcice
Bobrek/Oścwięcim
Brunn/Brno
Budy
Charlottegrube/Rydułtowy
Chełmek/Chełmek-Paprotnik
Chorzów
Chrzanów
Czernica
Eintrachthütte/Świętochłowice
Ernforst
Ernfort-Sławęcice
Freudenthal/Bruntál
Fürstengrube/Laski
Gleiwitz I, II, II, IV/Gliwice
Golleschau/Goleszów
Gunthergrubbe/Ledziny
Harmęże
Hindenburg/Zabrze
Hubertushütte-Hohenlinde/Łagiewniki
Janigagrube-Hoffnung/Libiąż
Jawischowitz
Kobio/Kobiór
Lagischa/ŁagiszaLaurahütte/Siemianowice
Lepziny-Lawki
Lesslau-Włocławek
Libiąż Mały
Łuków
Monowitz/Monowice
Mysłowice
Neu Dachs/Jaworzno
Neustadt/Prudnik
Pławy
Rajsko
Rybnik
Rydułtowy
Siemianowice
Sosnowitz I and II/Sosnowiec
Trzebinia
Tscechwitz/Czechowice
Włocławek/Leslau
Zasole
Zittau
Belzec (extermination camp – 1 sub-camp)
Izbica
Bierznow
Biesiadka
Dzierżązna & Litzmannstadt
Gross-Rosen – Rogoźnica (77 sub-camps)
Aslau
Bad Warmbrunn/Cieplice
Bautzen
Berndorf/Bernartice
Blechhammer
Bolkenhain/Bolków
Breslau/Wrocław
Brief/Brzeg

Brünnlitz/Brněnec
Brusay/Brzezowa
Buchwald Höhenwöse
Bunzlau/Bolesławiec
Bunzlau-Rauscha/Ruszów
Christianstadt
Dornhau
Dyhernfurth/Brzeg Dolny
Erlenbusch
Eule
Falkenberg
Faulbruk
Frierland
Fürstenstein
Gabersdorf
Gassen
Gebhardsdorf/Giebułtów
Gellenau/Jeleniów
Görlitz
Graben
Granefort
Grulich/Králíky
Grünberg
Gruschwitz/Kruszwica
Halbstadt/Meziměstí
Hartmannsdorf
Hirschberg/Jelenia Góra
Hohenelbe/Vrchlabí
Kaltwasser
Kamenz
Kittlitztreben/Kotlicki-Trebin
Kurzbach Grunthal
Landeshut/Kamienogora
Langenbielau/Bielawa
L'Arche Ludwigsdorf
Lehmwasser
Leszno/Lissa
Mahrisch
Markstädt/Laskowice
Marzdorf/Martínkovice
Merzbachtal
Mittelsteine
Neisse-Neusalz Oder/Nowa Sól
Niesky
Niesky Klein

Niesky Wittischenau
Radisch
Oberalstadt
Oberwüstegiersdorf
Parschnitz/Porici
Peterswaldau
Prausnitz/Brusnica
Rauscha/Ruszów
Reichenau/Rzeszów
Reichenau Reichenbach
Reichenau Reichenberg Liberal
Schmiedeberg
Schotterwerk
Seuferwassergraben
Striegau/Strzegom
Tannhausen
Waldenburg
Weiswasser
Wolfsberg
Wustegierdorf/Giercze Puste
Wustegierdorf Station
Wüstewaltersdorf
Zittau
Czwartacki
Huta Komarowska
Janowska
Kraków
Kulmhof – Chełmno
(extermination camp – no sub-camp known)
Lemberg
Lublin (prison – no sub-camp known)
Lwów (Lemberg)
Majdanek (extermination camp – 3 sub-camps)
Budzyń
Hrubieszów
Lublin
Mielec
Pawiak (prison – no sub-camp known)
Płaszów (work camp, later a sub-camp of **Majdanek**)

Poniatowa
Pustków
Radogoszcz
Radom
Schmolz/Smolec
Schokken/Skoki
Sobibor
Stutthof – Sztutowo
(40 sub-camps)
Bocień
Bromberg
Brusy
Chorabie
Cieszyny
Danzig-Burggraben/Kokoszki
Danzig-Neufahrwasser
Danzigerwerf/Gdańsk
Dzimianen
Elbing/Elbląg
Gdynia
Gendorf
Gerdenau
Graudenz
Grodno
Gutowo
Gwiździny
Heiligenbeil
Jessu
Kokoschken
Kolkau
Krzemieniewo
Lauenburg
Malken Mierzynek
Nawitz
Niskie
Obrzycko
Prault
Pruszcz
Rosenberg/Brodnica
Scherokopas
Schiffenbeil
Serappen
Sophienwalde
Slipsk
Stargorod
Szczecin/StettinToruń

Treblinka
Wieliczka
Żabikowo (work camp – no sub-camp known)
Zakopane

Russia
Akmétchetka
Bar
Baranówka
Bisjumujsje
Bogdanovka
'Citadelle'
Czwartacki
Daugavpils
Domanivka
Edineti
Khorol
Kielbasin (or Kelbassino)
Klooga
Lemberg
Mežaparks
Ponary
Rawa Ruska
Salaspils
Strazdumujsje
Vertigen
Yanowski (for all these camps, no sub-camp known)

Yugoslavia
Banjica
Bročice
Chabatz
Đakovo
Danica
Gornja Reka
Gradiška
Jadovno
Jasenovac
Jastrebarsko
Kragujevac
Krapje
Kruščica
Lepoglava
Loborgrad
Sajmište
Sisak
Slano
Slavonska-Požega
Stara Gradiška
Tašmajdan
Zemun

Appendix II

Auschwitz Sub-Camps

Operational between 1942 and 1944

Altdorf
  Stara Wieś near Pszczyna (1942 to 1943)
  Forest detail
  10–20 prisoners

Althammer
  Stara Kuźnia near Halemba (September 1944 to January 1945)
  Construction of thermal electric power plant
  486 prisoners

Babitz
  Babitz near Auschwitz (March 1943 to January 1945)
  Agricultural work (SS farm)
  159 male prisoners and approximately 180 female prisoners

Birkenau
  Birkenau (1943 to January 1945)
  Farming and agricultural duties (SS farm)
  204 male prisoners

Bismarckhütte
  Chorzów (September 1944 to January 1945)
  Production of military vehicles and naval guns at Bismarck Mill

Blechhammer
  Sławięcice near Blachownia Śląska (April 1944 to January 1945)
  Construction of chemical plant
  157 female prisoners

Bobrek
  Bobrek near Auschwitz (May 1944 to January 1945)
  Production of electrical aircraft and submarine parts
  38 female prisoners

Brunn
  Brno (Czechoslovakia) (October 1943 to January 1945)
  Construction work on the SS and Police Technical Academy
  250 prisoners

Budy
  Near Auschwitz (April 1942 to January 1945)
  Agricultural labour (SS farm)
  313 prisoners

Budy
Near Auschwitz (June 1942 to spring 1943)
Farming (SS farm), forced labour including drainage ditches and cleaning and deepening of fish ponds
300–400 female prisoners (penal company)

Budy
Near Auschwitz (April 1943 to autumn 1944)
Agricultural labour (SS farm)
600–800 female prisoners

Buna (*aka* Monowitz-Buna and Auschwitz III)
Synthetic rubber production plant IG Farben
10,000–12,000 male and female prisoners

Charlottegrube
Rydułtowy (September 1944 to January 1945)
Coal-mining and mine construction work (Hermann Göring Werke)
833 prisoners

Chełmek
Chełmek (October 1942 to December 1942)
Shoe factory and work detail also including cleaning water reservoir
150 prisoners

Eintrachthütte
Świętochłowice (May 1943 to January 1945)
Production of anti-aircraft artillery (Eintracht mill)
1,297 prisoners

Freudental
Bruntalu (Protectorate of Bohemia and Moravia) (1944 to January 1945)
Fruit processing
301 female prisoners

Fürstengrube
Wesoła near Mysłowice (September 1943 to January 1945)
Coal-mining (Fürsten mine)
1,283 prisoners

Gleiwitz II
Gliwice (March 1944 to January 1945)
Repair of railways and rolling stock
1,336 prisoners (17 January 1945)

Gleiwitz II
Gliwice (May 1944 to January 1945)
Production of coal tar including maintenance of machinery
740 male and 371 female prisoners

Gleiwitz III
Gliwice (July 1944 to January 1945)
Construction work on Gleiwitzer Hütte factory building plus by-production of arms, ammunition and railway wheels
609 prisoners

Gleiwitz IV
Gliwice (June 1944 to January 1945)
Barracks construction and repair including repair of military vehicles
444 prisoners

Golleschau
Goleszów (July 1942 to January 1945)
SS cement plant
1,008 prisoners

Günthergrube
Lędziny (February 1944 to January 1945)
Coal-mining (Piast mine)
586 prisoners

Harmense
Harmęże near Auschwitz (December 1941 to summer 1943)
Farming (SS farm) including raising and caring for poultry, rabbits and fish
70 prisoners

Harmense
Harmęże near Auschwitz (June 1942 to January 1945)
Farming (SS farm) including raising and caring for poultry, rabbits and fish
50 female prisoners

Hindenburg
Zabrze (August 1944 to January 1945)
Armaments (Donnersmarck mill)
470 female prisoners

Hubertushütte
Łagiewniki (December 1944 to January 1945)
Labour gangs (Hubertus mill)
202 prisoners

Janinagrube
Libiąż (September 1943 to January 1945)
Coal-mining (Janina mine)
853 prisoners

Jawischowitz
Jawiszowice (August 1942 to January 1945)
Coal-mining and construction work at the Brzeszcze-Jawischowitz mine
1,988 prisoners

Kobier
Kobiór (1942 to 1943)
Forestry work (Pszczyna forestry authority)
158 prisoners

Lagischa
Łagisza (September 1943 to September 1944)
Construction of the Walther thermal electric power plant
1,000 prisoners

Laurahütte
Siemianowice (April 1944 to January 1945)
Production of anti-aircraft artillery (Laura mill)
937 prisoners

Lichtewerden
Světlá (Protectorate of Bohemia and Moravia) (November 1944 to January 1945)
Thread factory
300 female prisoners

Mesersitz
Międzyrzecze (October 1942 to January 1943)
Forestry work

Neu-Dachs
Jaworzno (June 1943 to January 1945)
Coal-mining (Jaworzno mines and construction of the Wilhelm electric power plant)
3,664 prisoners

Neustadt
Prudnik (September 1944 to January 1945)
Textile mill
399 female prisoners

Plawy
Pławy near Auschwitz (1944 to January 1945)
Farming (SS farm)
138 male and 200 female prisoners

Radostowitz
Radostowice near Pszczyna (1942 to 1943)
Forestry work
20 prisoners

Raisko
Rajsko (June 1943 to January 1945)
Farming (SS farm) including gardening
300 female prisoners

Sonderkommando Kattowitz
Katowice (January 1944 to January 1945)
Construction of air-raid shelters and barracks for the Gestapo
10 prisoners

Sosnowitz (I)
Sosnowiec (August 1943 to February 1944)
Repairs of an office building
100 prisoners

Sosnowitz (II)
Sosnowiec (May 1944 to January 1945)
Casting barrels for anti-aircraft cannon and producing shells (Steel Mill)
863 prisoners

Sosnitz
Near Gliwice (July-August 1940)
Demolition of buildings at the site of a PoW camp
30 prisoners

SS Bauzug
   Karlsruhe (September to October 1944)
   Clearing rubble and repairing railway lines in the city
   500 prisoners

SS Hütte Porombka
   Międzybrodzie (October/November 1940 to January 1945)
   Construction and staffing of an SS rest house
   5–10 female prisoners

Trzebinia
   Trzebinia (August 1944 to January 1945)
   Expansion of the refinery (Erdöl Rafinerie)
   641 prisoners

Tschechowitz (I)
   Czechowice Dziedzice (August to September 1944)
   Removal of unexploded bombs from the refinery and surrounding areas
   100 prisoners

Tschechowitz (II)
   Czechowice Dziedzice (September 1944 to January 1945)
   Clearing rubble and maintaining the refinery
   561 prisoners

Notes